free from fear

For distribution, contact and ordering information,
please refer to the last page of this book.

© Copyright 2003 by Rev. J. W. Arnold
ISBN # 0-9740922-9-0

All rights reserved. No part of this book may be
reproduced in any form without written permission
from Rev. J. W. Arnold.
The Pentecostals of Gainesville
8105 NW 23rd Avenue
Gainesville, FL 32606
(352) 376-6320
www.gainesvilleupc.net

<u>Free From Fear</u>

Transcribed from the audiotape
series originally titled:
"Set Free From Fear"

A BookEnds Press Publication
PO Box 14513
Gainesville, FL 32604

free from fear
Chapter One

God Wants Me Totally Free	1
Not A Social Gospel	2
First Get The Spirit Right	4
Beware of Being Taken Captive	5
The Original Captives Brought a Curse	6
Who Is Upside Down—You or Them	7
Life & Liberty—Twins of the Gospel	7
Truth is a Person—More Than a Doctrine	8
Only The Spirit of Truth Leads to Truth	9
Your Word is the Expression of You	10
God Wants us Free in All Areas of Life	12
The Reason God Wants us Free	12
Let Perfect Love Operate	13
God's Desire—Fear Not	14
Fear—Our Greatest Problem	14
Our Thoughts—The Birthplace of Fear	15
Fear and Faith Activates Our Emotions	16
You Become What You Think	16
The Path of Thoughts—From Mind to Heart	17
Faith Pleases God—Fear Pleases Satan	18
Don't Fear Man—Fear God	18
What Begins as a Way Becomes Error, Then Rebellion	20
Determining Faith or Fear	21
The Law of Attraction	21
From Our Head to Our Heart-Emotions Are Activated	21
David—A Good Example of Faith & Fear	23
The Sin is Not in Being Afraid—It's Staying Afraid	23
When Fear Grips, Run—To The Throne	24
Faith—The Antidote For Fear	25

Chapter Two

The Holy Ghost—Old Testament vs. New Testament	27
What's Been Promised Must be Performed	28
Performance Then Brings Fulfillment	28
Fear is an Alien Emotion	29
Actions That Violate Revealed Will Produce Guilt and Guilt Brings Fear	30
God is Not a Tyrant	31
Faith, Not Emotions, Says God Loves Us	31
Trespass & Violated Knowledge Produce Fear	32
Misuse of God's Vessel (Our Body) is a Trespass	33
People Need Relief—Not Rules	33
Fear is Produced in Many Ways	34
Fear is Produced When we Violate Knowledge	35
The Only Work of Fear is Torment	37
Faith—The Antidote For Fear	38
God Delivers Us From Fear—Not Always the Situation	38
Changing Location Doesn't Dispel Fear, Because Every Where You Go, There You Are	39
Take Fear to the Throne	40
God Gives Peace in the Situation	41
Who Gives the Spirit of Fear?	42
Spirit of Fear Cast Out With Words	43
What's Been Cast Out Must be Replaced	43
Replace Fear With Things of God	44
No Fear—No Oppression	45
WE ARE the Righteousness of God	45
Satan, The Accuser	46
Peace With God	46
Ignorance, The Unexplained & Unknown Cause Fear	47
We Need the Word—Not Reason	49
Release What's Inside With Words	49
Fear Breeds Unbelief	50
You Gotta Learn to Fight	51
The Things of God Are Spiritually Discerned	51
Why Speaking in Tongues Rejected by Many	52
Satan's Greatest Tool—Fear—From Seeing Pictures in Your Mind and Feeling Them	52
Overcome Fear With Knowledge & Experience	53
Destroy the Seed Before it Takes Root	54

Chapter Three

Faith Only Come From God's Word	55
Confidence in the Lord Being Your Light & Life	56
Fear, Worry & Anxiousness—The Three Faced Evil	57
Fear—The First Negative Emotion in Mankind	58
"It Is Written"—Not All You Need	59
We Need the Power of the Author	60
Negative Response—Bondage—Captivity—Torment	60
Your Level of Knowledge Produces Your Response	61
Partial Knowledge is Dangerous	62
Again: The Bible Has a Years Worth of "Fear Not"	64
God Puts us in the Middle to Show us it Won't Hurt	64
Fear Resists Rationale	65
Be Transformed—Renew Your Mind	65
Time For a Recharge	66
We Gravitate to, and Become, What Our Mind Picture	67
Mental Pictures Produce Feelings; Feelings—Behavior	68
Fear Causes God to Drop the Shield	69
Our Brain Lies To Us	70
Faith Comes *Only* Through Hearing The Word of God	71
The Answer: Replace Fear Image With Faith Picture	72
God Replaces the Eliezer Picture in Abraham's Mind	73
Fill Your Mind With Faith Images	75
Either the Problem or Promise Will Produce Picture	76
No One Escapes the Onslaught of Fear	76
The Antidote for Worry—Work	77
Forget the Past—Create A Faith Image	78
See Yourself As.... Rather Than *Feeling*	79
See the End Result in Your Mind	80
Faith Images For Any Time of the Day or Night	81
David Was Fearful But Overcame	81
Opposed While Working up Faith Image	82
God Helps in Trying Times	82

Chapter Four

Peace God's Way—In the Midst of Trouble	85
Peace in Tribulation	86
Fear Producers—Ignorance, The Unknown, The Unfamiliar and the Adverse	87
Three Results of Satanic Fear	88
Two Types of Fear—Satanic & Godly	89
The Result of Rebellion—Fear	89
Doubt—Faith in the Enemy	90
The Fear of the Lord Brings Comfort	90
Satanic Fear Chokes Out Love	91
Divine Love Cannot be Demonstrated Where Satanic Fear Is In Place	92
Fear, Being a Spirit, Has Personality	93
Only Spirits Can be Cast Out	94
The Three 'C's' To Victory: *Cast* Out Spirits—*Crucify* Flesh—*Confess* Sin	94
It's Not the Devil—It's Flesh	96
You Will do for Gold What You Won't for God	96
Spiritual Problems Can Produce Sickness	97
Living in Obedience to God Negates the Devil's Torment	98
Godly Fear Brings Liberty	99
Two Fears—One Dominates, The Other Liberates	99
Fear of God—Reverence—Brings Comfort	100
Only the Fear of the Lord Brings Comfort	101
The Importance of a Daily Prayer Life	102
Don't Struggle—It's Easy to Live for God	103
Live Comfortably in the Holy Ghost	103
God's Purpose—Save You and Others Through You	104
You Cannot Inherit What Faith Gives Until You Overcome What Fear Produces	105
What You Don't Overcome Dominates You	105
Obey the Word—Leave the Results to God	106
Jesus Said, "Fear Not"	106

Chapter Five

Fear Will Come, But Don't Be Dominated By It	109
Stir Up The *Gift* to Combat Fear	110
God Can Do What We Can't	111
Don't Be Ashamed—But Be Partaker—of Afflictions of The Gospel	112
Overcoming Fear	113
Let The Love of God Overcome Fear	113
We Need to be Filled With Love of God	114
Fear Has Many Relatives	115
Unforgiveness Brings Torments	115
Take Inventory—Who Do I Need to Forgive	116
Want to be Like Jesus—Start With Forgiving Others	117
Peace Born Out of a Forgiving Heart	118
Forgive and Forget!	118
Just Let it Go!	119
God's Love Not Predicated on Performance	120
Being Like Jesus is a Journey	121
Walk in the Light—It Shows What We Need to Change	122
The Deep Things of God is Brighter Light	123
To Overcome Fear Fill Mind With Thoughts of God	123
Direction Needed With Emotional Experience	124
Use Scripture as Preventive Medicine—Not A Cure-all	125
Don't Live Borderline	126
Fill Your Mind With Thoughts of God	126
Quality Over Quantity in Scripture Reading	127
Fill Your Head With Fear or Faith—Word of the Enemy or Word of God	127
Be Transformed by Renewing Mind	128
Full of Holy Ghost Energy But Frustrated	129
Think on These Things....	129
God's Word—From Your Eyes & Ears to Your Heart	130
Faith & Fear—Both From Seeing & Hearing	131
Faith Should Grow From What's Seen & Heard of God	132
Bro. Arnold's closing remarks	135

Chapter One

God Wants Me Totally Free

I want to start this series and I want to just talk on "God wants me totally free." God has opened my brain and let me see some things I have never seen. God wants me totally free. Psalm 56:1-2 "Be merciful unto me, O God: for man would swallow me up; he fighting daily oppreseth me. Mine enemies would daily swallow me up: for they be many that fight against me, O thou most High." You need to underline this next verse in your Bible. It needs to become the criteria for your life.

Verse 3: "What time I am afraid, I will trust in thee." Verse 4-13 "In God will I praise His word, in God have I put my trust; I will not fear what flesh can do unto me. Every day they wrest my words: all their thoughts are against me for evil. They gather themselves together, they hide themselves, they mark my steps, when they wait for my soul. Shall they escape by iniquity? In thine anger cast down the people, O God. Thou tellest my wanderings: put thou my tears into thy bottle: are they not in thy book? When I cry unto thee, then shall mine enemies turn back: this I know; for God is for me. In God will I praise His word; In the Lord will I praise his word. In God have I put my trust. I will not be afraid what man can do unto me. Thy vows are upon me, O god: I will render praises unto thee. For thou hast delivered my soul from death: wilt thou not deliver my feet from falling, that I may walk before God in the light of the living?"

And one more scripture in Luke 4:17: "And there was delivered unto him the book of the prophet Esaias. And when he had opened the book, he found the place where it was written. 'The Spirit of the Lord is upon me, because he hath anointed me to preach the Gospel to the poor; He hath sent me to heal the brokenhearted, to preach deliverance to the captives, and recovering of sight to the blind, to set at liberty them that are bruised. Preach the acceptable year of the Lord.'"

It's always been an interesting portion of scripture in Luke 4, when the Lord constantly said again and again, "The Spirit of the Lord is upon me, because he has anointed me for a task." And then he tells us what the task is. He says, " I am to preach the good news to the poor. And I have been sent to heal the brokenhearted." Please notice now… " I am to preach to the poor, to help the poor."

Not A Social Gospel

Now that's not a social gospel like you hear today. That's not what it was. He didn't set up the YMCA when he was doing this. The gospel's not a social gospel—it's spiritual kingdom truth. He said, "I have come to heal the broken hearted." A person who is brokenhearted is emotionally crushed. And so why we, many times, exalt the magnitude of the Lords healing ministry for the physical man, He said, "One of these steps in my platform, as Gods anointed preacher, is to heal the brokenhearted, those who are hurting inside. Those who are hurting in places that only I the Lord know, because I deal in secret things." And he said, "I've come to preach deliverance to the captives. And to set at liberty them that are bruised."

You only get a bruise when you bump into something unintentionally. He can actually say that I've come to help those who got bumped into. It didn't say an open wound; it said a bruise. If you just get hit by something, or bump into something, about a day or two later you got a big purple, orange, red and green looking thing, and boy what a bruise. Well, I'll tell you something; the hurt was underneath the surface. It just took a couple days to rise.

When you see a bruised piece of fruit, know this, the fruit's damaged way below the surface. The only reason you know it's bruised is that it finally surfaces. But there are people that go among us that are bruised all the time, but it hasn't shown up yet. That's why it's so important for us to be sensitive to peoples needs. And the Lord went around saying: "I've come to set the captives free. I'm coming to help those that are bruised, those who have been beat up and jostled up, knocked around. I've come to help those recover who are blind."

Then He says, "I've come to preach the acceptable year of the Lord." That is the year of jubilee. That means, "I've come to restore what's been lost. I've come to help people get back what used to be theirs." Now just stay with me here...Jesus Christ has to be the ultimate liberator. He actually came to liberate people. And man is a three-part being; soul, spirit, and body. And when Paul writes one of his epistles to one of the churches he says, "I pray that you may be kept that you could present your soul, spirit and body, in that day." And unless the church ministers to that three-fold being, we're out of kilter. For to be able to have faith to anoint with oil in the name of the Lord Jesus, and release faith so they could be healed physically while they're carrying a bruise, or while they are brokenhearted, what good would their physical healing be, when inside they're an emotional wreck? And the heart of the Gospel is to first get the spirit right, because the spirit died.

First Get The Spirit Right

When Adam sinned and transgressed, the spirit died within a man. It didn't leave him; he's a spirit to begin with. All that happened was that he stepped from the spiritual plain into the soulish plain, so that now his soul, which is his will, his intellect, his emotion, now operates the body. That's why people respond to music; it's soulish. And as long as the soul is in charge, the body will do dumb things. But when you're regenerated, (that means to start something up that used to run [regenerated]) then the spirit comes alive and now the spirit will govern what the body does, because the spirit will govern with a criteria of control—the human emotion.

That's why sometimes, if you can accept this, sometimes our worship is soulish. We're beat-oriented, and I'm not against beat, but somewhere in that beat, somewhere in that quick or slow tempo, we've got to leave the soulish realm…you don't have to be a spiritual giant to know that I'm telling you the truth. Then there are times when we'll just worship Him as we're suppose to, and then all of a sudden you can tell; you'll go, "Whew, I feel the power of God." What's happened? You've left soul; now you're spirit. Yes, you can sense it like that if you have an ounce of the Holy Ghost. Now we're in the spirit realm. Now the impossible becomes possible. And as long as you function in the soulish realm, frustration is possible.

You can scream at devils and pray and curse sickness all you want, but that soulish realm is just emotion, will and intellect. But if you can somehow just get through that door and step into that spirit realm, in a second, virtue can fall. That's what happens. Sometimes we just step up into that plane, and a lot of us know when we step back out of it. God's truth. So I want to talk to you for a little while.

Beware of Being Taken Captive

Captives. What a word. Captives: People who are taken prisoner against their will. Invaded by an alien force or power. Captured against their own choosing. No power within them to remain free, as they want to. They just become captured. Various governments now in our news, take over day by day. And those that are not slain are then put in prison, or sent away. What are they? They're captives. They've been overrun and overtaken by a force greater than them without their choosing. We've done it all through life. That's what wars are all about. That's how prisoner-of-war camps came. That's how geography was divided up after Berlin and after the Second World War. We took things captive. You can take land captive. You can take people captive. And you can take economies captive. In fact, you can take it down to the lower level and just ride out here to 39th avenue and we've got a jail out there and those people are "captives." They've been taken prisoners against their wills.

At the beginning, man and his environment were free; totally. There was no ecology problem. God's atmosphere was pure. There was no problem with Adam and Eve; they were totally free. They didn't have to get into the spirit; they were always in the spirit. That's why Paul talks about living in the spirit. Why? You may not be able to wait until Sunday and you need God now. And you can be washing the dishes, or cleaning the house, or driving your car, but if you're in the spirit then you literally can constantly have a communication with you and your God, and you don't have to spend thirty minutes to get a hold of God. You can say, "Jesus!"

I'm going to tell you, there have been times in my life when I've said that, and I've felt the response from the Lord. That's why it's absolute spiritual tragedy for people to be carnal and claim themselves Christians. Because that means you have to have twenty or thirty minutes to warm up. You may have three seconds to stop that car. I'm going to tell you again friend, I may be your pastor, but I can't be your spiritual guru. You need to be your own. You're a priest. You need to be able to just communicate with God.

The Original Captives Brought a Curse

So, they were enjoying life, they were enjoying the atmosphere and they were enjoying God. Satan tempted them. You know the story. Eve responded, and when she responded, trespass took Eve and Adam captive. They don't want to be captives, but they are. Now, because of that trespass it brought a curse on the land. It brought a curse on the human body. It was never sick before sin. It brought a curse on the spiritual life; his spirit ceased to function with God. He was now a soulish man living in a body. He would do what our generation says, "If it feels good, do it." That's soul talking.

The problem with living in the soul realm is that the soul doesn't have any rules. The only thing that can govern the soul of men and women is spirit. But if the spirit is unregenerate and dead, then the soul is in charge. That's why you have drug addicts. That's why you have murderers. That's why you have drunks…their soul rules.

Trespass took them captive and spirit died and the soul ruled. To a slave, liberty is like Heaven. Liberty is like a dream come true. To some, though, who have never been free, listen carefully, it is easy to adapt to the lifestyle of a slave. …You know nothing else.

Who Is Upside Down—You or Them

That is why in the book of Acts it was recorded, when Paul and his crew came in, they said, "These are they that have turned the world upside-down." Here's why they said that; because ever since they had lived on this planet they had lived upside-down, and when you live upside-down, right side-up looks upside-down. That's why, when you witness to people and testify about the Holy Ghost, talking in tongues, water baptism in Jesus name and a pure clean holy life, they look at you and go, " Huh?" Why? They were born upside-down. They're out of communion with God. They have no spiritual balance and no spiritual perception. And so when they look at you, you look upside-down.

Why doesn't the world just respond to this great Gospel message? They're upside-down. And here you come walking in and you don't fit. Everybody in their world walks upright, and here you come walking in and they're like, "What's wrong with you?" Nothing wrong with me: I've got the Holy Ghost. I'm baptized in Jesus name. I live clean, holy and godly...nothing wrong with me. What's wrong with you?

Life & Liberty—Twins of the Gospel

What is the Gospel supposed to do? Turn people, right! Profound.... Those who were born slaves never miss liberty; they never tasted it. They don't even know what it is; don't even desire it. And our world has experienced many, many liberators. There was a gentleman in the revolution named Patrick Henry who said, "Give me liberty or give me death." If I understand what Mr. Henry said, then liberty must be life, and bondage and captivity must be death. He said he'd rather die than not have liberty.

But if I have liberty, then I've got life. If I live without liberty, I'm just existing. I'm really dead. Stay with me now. Jesus said with his own mouth in John 10, "I've come that you might have life and have it more abundantly." How was Jesus going to bring the human race life? Easy, he would share with them truth. It was in John 8 that Jesus said, "Ye shall know the truth and the truth shall make you free." It'll set you free. What liberates? Truth! What captivates? Error! He turned to those Jews and said: Man, I'm telling you what; you shall know the truth and the truth shall make you free.

And they said, "We ain't never been slaves to nobody." I've often wondered about these idiots…I keep wanting to ask, "What was that four hundred year stint in Egypt, a cruise?" …"we've never been slaves to anybody…." WHAT? What was Pharaoh; your uncle? Could you imagine Jesus looking at these men when they said, "We've never been in bondage, or slaves, or servitude to any man." Huh? "What was Egypt?" " Oh, we was just farming."

Truth *is a Person—More Than a Doctrine*

Notice please, carefully, the wording. He did not say, "You shall know *about* the truth." He said, "Ye shall know the *truth*." Why? Because the *truth* is a person. Jesus said, "I am the truth."

So watch what he says, "Ye shall know the truth and the truth…." …now we've had our boasts for years, "Well, I know the truth…." What we were saying is; we knew a set of cardinal doctrines that we believe. That ain't set us free yet! We still got adulterers and we still got liars and we still got frustrated people, but you find people in the midst of that camp that KNOW the TRUTH; they're free! They're not under condemnation. They're not in bondage. They're not captive of their emotions and attitudes. No; because when you know the truth, the truth sets you free. Let me go a little further here. Not only is the truth a person; the truth is a spirit. He said in John 14:16-18, "I'm going to pray the Father and he shall send you another Comforter... even the Spirit of truth. Which in whom the world can not receive, because it seeth him not." It doesn't know him!

Now you got to get this folks, because the Spirit of *truth* is a Him. We're always referring to the Holy Ghost as an "it." You get "it." You don't get "it." You get Him. Jesus said when "He" the Spirit of truth has come. The Spirit of truth is a *he*. ...Going to reprove the world for this, that, and the other thing. ...Bring to remembrance things that I told you. ...And he will lead you and guide you into all truth.

Only The Spirit of Truth Leads to Truth

That's why it's stupid for any kind of church, and I don't care what label they have on their door, that says, "Bless God, we don't believe in the Holy Ghost talking in tongues." You're an idiot, because the only thing that's going to take you into all truth is the Spirit of truth! He just told you that you couldn't learn that. God is a self-revealing deity and He reveals himself through His Word and the anointing of His Spirit that makes His Word LIFE! But without the Spirit, the letter killeth! But the Spirit makes it alive! That's why people who study for years in Seminaries and read books and write books don't know beans! And I'm not being derogatory to any of these precious men and women who have dedicated their lives to study and writing and what-have-you, but this stuff is revealed to us by the Spirit.

The Bible says, "Eye hath not seen, nor ear heard, neither have entered into the heart of man the things which God has prepared for them that love Him." Now we usually stop there. The next verse is very important. "But God hath revealed them...." What's the them? The things that our eyes have not seen, the ears not heard..., but God has revealed them unto us by His Spirit. Why? Because God is truth, and His Spirit reveals Him to us.

"Well I don't believe in the Holy Ghost," Well you're missing some wonderful, grand something from God that could help you understand. That's why we have ten thousand different so-called Christian doctrines. It's because well meaning men and women who study and do pray, but are not spiritual, interpret this from the intellectual and soul platform. And I'll tell you what, the reason they're more popular than I am is that the people that they deal with are on the same plane. And rationale and reason says that makes sense.

Your Word is the Expression of You

In Hebrews 4, where it talks about, "the Word of God is quick, powerful, and sharper than a two-edged sword, dividing asunder, the spirit, the soul, the marrow of the bone...." Remember that? For years I heard that preached and taught, and thought it was the Word of God. But if you go down to the next verse it says, "Neither is any creature not naked, not manifest in His sight." Well now then, the Word of God is a person. I'll prove it to you. In Revelation, we see Jesus with many crowns on His head sitting on that horse, and his vest is dipped in blood. And on the side of His thigh it says "The Word of God." You know what a word is? When you and I say a word, you know what that is? Your word isn't separate from you. Your word is a declaration of you. It's a manifestation of your thought and feeling. But you couldn't say, "Now he gave me his word. Now I got his word and that's one person and he's another person."

A man or a woman...their word is one. All a word is is a manifestation of thought. That's why the Bible says, John 1:1, "In the beginning was the Word and the Word was with God and the Word was God and the Word was manifest that we saw Jesus." What? That he was the Word of God? He is God's thought? God's purpose? God's heart in a body? My, my, my! So the word *is* a person....
And the Bible says, "And the Word is Spirit and the Word is life." Jesus said, "That when He the Comforter is come" ...watch... "whom the world cannot receive because it seeth Him not, neither knoweth Him, but you know Him" ...not "it," but Him...for "He" ...not "it," but "He" ..."dwelleth with you and shall be in you." Paul just throws the whole thing together in one verse and says I'll end the whole dispute about the Godhead: "Christ in you the hope of glory."

Now I know who the *Holy Ghost* is. Now I know who the *He* is. Now I know who the *world* is. Now I know who the *comforter* is. "Know ye not that ye are the temple of the Holy Ghost." You've become Heaven's house.

Listen carefully. Therefore, Jesus said he would set people free by the truth. The Son would make you free. You ever put those two verses together; in John 8:32 to about John 8:36? First, he says the truth shall set you free and then he goes up about five verses and says; if the Son makes you free, you're free indeed. Notice he says the truth will set you free and then the Son will make you free. Something tells me the *truth* is the *Son*. We ain't got two forces trying to do the same thing. We got one force.

free from fear

God Wants us Free in All Areas of Life

God wants us free in every area of our lives. Therefore, he grants unto us knowledge that frees us from ignorance. He grants us truth that frees us and liberates us from error and falsehood. He grants us experiences that sets us free form suppositions, suspicion and apprehension. And then God gives us His Spirit, because the Bible says that Spirit is life, which sets us free from death. That's why the Bible says if any men have not the Spirit of Christ, he's none of His. You've got no life in you.

The Reason God Wants us Free

Now listen very, very carefully. Here's the reason why God wants us free. 1 John 4:18, "There is no fear in love, but perfect love casteth out fear." I'm going to hit you hard now. You can't cast out an emotion. If you don't hear anything else I say, hear this. "The three C's." You *cleanse* sin, you *cast* out spirits, but you *crucify* flesh. For years, us holy rollers were trying to cast out flesh, and crucify spirits…I want you to let it settle for a while, because it's the key to revival. There are some things we have pleaded with God to deliver us from, that, in the first place, it wasn't a spirit; it was flesh. And the Bible says, "They that are in Christ have crucified the flesh with the lust thereof." And there are some things we've been trying to crucify that wasn't flesh, but spirits that needed to be cast out. And there've been other things in us that we've been trying to cast out and crucify, and neither one of them will work. You've got to cleanse it by the blood. You can't cleanse a devil! You'll see in a minute. "Because fear hath torment." That's why God wants us free. "Because fear hath torment."

You have children? Aren't you tormented when your offspring are tormented? Aren't you upset when they suffer? Aren't you beside yourself with anguish when someone that you know very dearly is terrified, or overwhelmed by a situation and no matter how you try to reason with them you cannot alleviate their fears? You know why? Because human reasoning and scripture quoting will do nothing for fear. It's a spirit. It demonstrates itself through human emotion. You feel fear? Sure you do. You feel the Holy Ghost? Sure you do. Why? They're both spirits. How do you register the Holy Ghost? Try emotion. How do you register the devil? Try emotion. "He that hath fear is not made perfect in love." Right.

Let Perfect Love Operate

Perfect love casteth out all fear. Now I wonder whom we can find who's got perfect love. Nobody! But I know someone who IS perfect love, and HE casteth out all fear! When His Spirit is allowed to operate in thee and me, then fear isn't allowed to stay. Wait a minute...so you don't get wiped out.... You can have a good dose of the Holy Ghost and fear visits you twenty times a day. But it isn't allowed to stay as long as perfect love is allowed to operate in you.

I'm going to show you something. Luke 1:67-74 "And his father Zacharias was filled with the Holy Ghost and prophesied saying, 'Blessed be the Lord God of Israel; for he hath visited and redeemed his people. And hath raised up a horn of salvation for us in the house of his servant David; As he spake by the mouth of his holy prophets, which have been since the world began: that we should be saved from our enemies.'" This man's prophesying. That means the Spirit's talking through him. It ain't just Zechariahs writing up a little letter. The Spirit is talking through him... "And from the hand of all that hate us; to perform the mercy promised to our fathers." They've been given promises and now their going to get the performance of it... "And to remember his holy covenant; the oath which he sware to our father Abraham, that he would grant unto us, that we being delivered out of the hand of our enemies might serve him without fear." I read this thing for twenty years and I've missed that word. And most of you just missed it: "'without fear' that we could be delivered out of the hand of our enemies, that we could serve him without fear, In holiness and righteousness before him all the days of our life."

God's Desire—Fear Not

And God wants you to be free from fear. Why? Because fear hath torment. Fear produces anguish, anxiety, apprehension, tight neck muscles, stomach problems, fidgeting, reacting unkindly, and becoming somewhat critical.

I found this out and I didn't even know it: Do you know that recorded in our Bible, this term "fear not" and this one "neither be dismayed"; those terms are recorded in this Bible three hundred and sixty-six times? That's one "fear not" for every day of a leap year. Now I want that to settle, because you ain't got it yet. God, because we are His kids and He knows that fear hath torment, He gave us three hundred and sixty-six statements of "fear not, neither be dismayed."

Fear—Our Greatest Problem

Somehow, God is trying to address the greatest problematic issue with the human species. I'm telling you, it's the greatest problem we have. Fear is the strongest spirit that you will ever have to overcome. It is the first negative emotion mankind ever experienced. When he was in the garden, before he felt hate, jealousy, strife, envy, anger...mankind drank deep from "I was afraid." What brought the fear? Trespass brought guilt, and guilt gives birth to fear. There's only one cure that I've found so far in these scriptures for fear. The Bible says in Psalms 34:4; "I sought the Lord and he heard me and delivered me from all my fears." There's only one thing that can deliver anyone from fear, and that's the righteousness of God. Because once you're righteous with God, fear cannot dominate you. Isaiah 26:3 says; "Thou wilt keep him in perfect peace, whose mind is stayed upon thee for he trusteth in thee." Well, I ain't never heard anyone preach and teach this, so bear with me a second.

Our Thoughts—The Birthplace of Fear

I'm going to give you a question: Where does fear come from? That was real easy in Adam's case. It came from a trespass that produced guilt, and he was afraid, because he knew better. But how does all the rest of fear just somehow arrive at our door uninvited? ...Comes to us in the middle of the night. ...Doing the best you can for God. You haven't cursed, you haven't been immoral, you haven't been a drunk, you haven't been a fool and all of a sudden you turn around and fear says, "Hi!" I think I got the answer: Fear comes to us from our thoughts.

You know why I know that? Because that's exactly how faith comes. Faith cannot come to you directly into your hearts; it's got to go through your head. "Faith cometh by hearing and hearing by the word of God." When you hear the Word of God, your mind grabs hold of it and you either accept it, or reject it. If you accept it, faith goes "whoosh." If you reject it, you have no faith. That's why God chose, through the foolishness of preaching, to save them that believe.

Fear and Faith Activates Our Emotions

Why not just give everybody the Holy Ghost that needs the Holy Ghost? Because He's got to use the human mind. Philippians 4:7, "And the peace of God that passeth all understanding" …All understanding… "shall keep your hearts and minds through Christ Jesus." Yes. "Finally brethren whatsoever things are true…." Did you hear what he just said? "The peace of God that passeth all understanding will keep your hearts and minds;" because if your heart gets fearful it's because your brain got fearful. If your brain stops an episode it will never reach your heart. If some thought is given to you and your mind says, "Not so," it can go no further. It's like a trap door. That's right! Human will. It just says, "No!" But if your mind says, "I receive it," then your mind becomes affected and your heart becomes affected with either fear, or faith. And how will you react? Via emotions. Don't you get it? Fear and faith is the catalyst that declares how your emotions react.

You Become What You Think

Don't you get why we're so angry about television and bad radio and bad literature that fills your mind with stuff, and you let that stuff get in your mind? The next stop is your heart! And Jesus said, "out of the heart proceedeth evil thoughts." Wait a minute…. How does a heart think? Well, God makes reference in the scripture about your heart and your soul; they're synonymous with each other. Talking about your will and your intellect and your emotion…"As a man thinks in his heart so is he." How can he think in his heart? The thought passed from his head! "Finally brethren whatsoever things are true, whatsoever things are honest, whatsoever things are just, whatsoever things are pure, whatsoever things are lovely, whatsoever things are of good report, if there be any virtue and if there be any praise, think on these things." Why? Because you'll become what you think. I'm telling you, the spirit of fear will come to anybody. And if you receive it and let it stay in your mind long enough, it'll move out of your mind and go to your heart.

The Path of Thoughts—From Mind to Heart

Your thoughts arise in your heart because they're in our heads. Why? "...because you're standing there, and we can't figure this out...you're supposed to be dead. We saw you get killed and you just came through the walls. That ain't normal!" Watch me. "What are you doing here? My mind says dead people don't talk and dead people don't walk." But there he is and the first thing he says is, "Hi fellows, peace be unto you." And they go "Whaaat?" Now watch. Their mind is going, "This can't be, this can't be, this is not right, this man is dead. This man is dead! Somebody's playing tricks on us. This man is not here." And so it leaves their head and fills their hearts. Why? Because the only way you can be saved is, "a man believes with his heart and confesses with his mouth," but it can't get to your heart until it does some work in your head.

You see, He says, "Why do thoughts arise in your hearts? Handle me and see." There's the key, folks! If you're full of fear, folks, it's because it's been a long time since you've *handled* the Word. If you handle the Word, fear hits the road! That's what He said. "Handle me and see." Which, in essence, is, "handle me and understand." If you read these two recordings, it says right after that, "And they were filled with gladness." When did gladness come? As soon as fear left! Soon as knowledge says, "This is God. This is

God. This is God." Fear hits the road. Joy and gladness come and…whooo! But as long as your brain intimidates you and says, "Uh-uh, uh-uh, uh-uh," you can do all you want to believe in your heart, but your head, friend, is stopping that heart from doing what you want it to do.

Faith Pleases God—Fear Pleases Satan

All through God's word, God says, "don't be afraid" three hundred and sixty-six times. Why does He say, "Don't be afraid"? Here's why; because fear can paralyze the greatest faith. And only faith pleases God. You ready for this? This is going to hurt a little bit, but hold on. Fear pleases Satan!

Take a deep breath now. Fear is no more, or less, than faith in the enemy. God said what the circumstance said, so you release fear and say, "You're lying!" Or you release faith and say, "No, you're lying!" Fear looks at the Word of God and says, "God won't, God can't and He shouldn't be trusted." Insult!

Don't Fear Man—Fear God

Well, we might as well learn. Jeremiah 1:8, "The Lord said to his prophets; fear not their faces." Why? Because the message you got is unpopular and you won't get either the Nobel Prize, or the Pulitzer Prize. But before He got His preachers started, He always got them lined up…and you read how many times He said to these prophets: "Now you listen, before you start preaching, hear what I'm going to tell you. Don't be afraid of their kisser, because they're going to look at you and stare you down and make faces and stick their tongue out and scrunch up their nose."

You think I'm kidding you? I know what it's like to sometimes preach here an unpopular theme, I watch the kisser. I'm almost better off with two hundred scumbags...just paint smiley faces on them and I'd say, "All right!" With everything I'd say, they'd be smiling.... I've preached enough revivals to know that some times I'd be used of the Holy Ghost to nail some people's hides to the wall to try and help them, and some people are happy when they're found in their sin; and some people would like to cut your guts out.

I remember preaching a meeting one time and turning around and saying, "Whoa, you got a nasty spirit about you." I'm mean, buddy...if she had a .357, I'd be going to paradise valley. I mean furious! "You know you got problems?" "Look at your face. The face is the indicator of the inward man."
"How do you know?"
"The Lord just told me. In fact, you're in adultery!"

...Big ol' tears start welling up.... "What's the matter with you? Sitting here playing the hypocrite, you dumb fool! ...going to die and go to a devil's Hell. What's the matter with you?"

I remember one time preaching a revival right here in this state, didn't know beans about the church, just went in there and all of a sudden the Lord gave me a message about Cora and Abiram and Dathan. I said, "What in the world is going on here?" I picked out a half a dozen people right in that church and didn't say anything out loud, I didn't want to embarrass them, walked over and said, "You're raising a bunch of "H" with your pastor." "Your giving him trouble ain't you?" "You got a bad spirit about you." "You're critical aren't you?"

What Begins as a Way Becomes Error, Then Rebellion

This is serious business, folks. This isn't a game. God doesn't take it lightly when people resist leadership. He may let people get by for a while, but I promise you, every one of them is going in the pit. Oh yes, it's the way of Canaan, the way of Cain…"my way is better than God's way." Then it becomes the error of Balaam. That means it's got more gold dust. Like these TV preachers got more gold dust than they got God. Then it finally ends up with Cora, and where does Cora go? …gets swallowed up alive and goes to the pit. First, it starts as a way, then it becomes an error, then it finally becomes open rebellion. The "gainsaying" of Cora. "Gainsaying" means open rebellion. They finally just stand against the man of God and say, "I'm just as holy as you, smart as you, and can quote scripture like you." You could probably do better, but you ain't the deputy. And before that was over, God just said, "Get back away from these boys. Watch this I'm going to do something new." And whoosh! I mean, families, kids, donkeys, everything went down there and got coughed back up; and fire come with a frenzy from the Lord and killed two hundred and fifty leaders of the camp; and He said, "Now we'll see who's working for who."

That scares the pudding out of me…scares the living daylights out of me. Terrifying. I don't like none of that. Ezekiel 3:9, "As an adamant harder than flint have I made thy forehead: fear them not." Joshua 1:9, "Be strong and be of good courage and be not afraid." God uses Words. Why? Because He is Spirit and we are spirit, but faith and fear come through the mind, because the mind weighs suggestions and words and then the mind sends a signal to the heart, and the heart sends a signal to the emotions, and therefore you either respond in agony, or joy in rejoicing, or resentment. You react, or you recoil.

Determining Faith or Fear

Israel saw and heard God descend on the mountain, but they became afraid of what they saw and heard. Moses saw and heard God and he responded positively in faith and walked into the cloud. Same demonstration in 2 Corinthians 10:3-5; the Bible talks about casting down imaginations and every high thing that exalts itself against the knowledge of God and bringing into captivity every thought to the obedience of Jesus Christ. What's he saying? The battleground is your brain. So we have to pull down strongholds. How we handle what we see and hear will determine whether we give birth to fear, or faith. Let me say again what David said, "What time I am afraid, I will trust in thee."

The Law of Attraction

Job 3:25 said, (this is powerful) "What I greatly feared came upon me." Now I ask a question: Why? Easy! The law of attraction. Listen to me. Job, even though he was a prosperous and a perfect man in his generation and one that feared the Lord and hated evil, yet somewhere in his thought life he was actually seeing some negative things happen. He said, "Finally the thing that I greatly feared has come upon me." Where did you get that fear, Job?

"I've been thinking about it. Some day I might lose my cattle and my kids might die, and I might get sick. I know I've had a great life, but I've just been thinking about it."

From Our Head to Our Heart—Emotions Are Activated

My God man, when you think about that stuff, you give birth to fear. And fear has torment. If we hold thoughts in our head long enough, they will get into our hearts. And that way our emotions are activated.

Listen to me, thoughts that are entertained become pictures and images of disaster, failure, and trouble. Job thought of going from prosperity to poverty, from health to sickness, therefore; the law of the harvest says he must receive what he sees. "Whereas the man thinketh, so is he."

Think for one more moment...David, the sweet Psalmist of Israel, who, through faith, whipped Goliath with all Israel viewing the same Goliath, and hearing the same thundering voice, responded in fear. And they're all in covenant with God! Yet, one sees and hears and gives birth to faith, and yet, another sees and hears and gives birth to fear! Why? It's how you handle the thought!

David said, "The Word of the Lord said no man can stand before us. Who's this uncircumcised Philistine? I'll go out and knock his ignorant head off." Why? "What time I am afraid I will trust in thee."

What did David say? "Well, he may be too big for me, but he ain't too big for you. Let's go!" You see, Saul and Israel...they couldn't say to God, "He's not too big for you!" because Saul was backslid. Saul had ceased to do anything right with God. And so now David's functioning and therefore he gives David his weaponry, he gives him his armament. "Here take this." That's what a soulish man would say. "We'll make the best out of the situation."

But the spiritual man would say, "I don't need this. I'm coming in the name of the Lord." Why? "Because what time I am afraid I will trust in thee and thou wilt keep me in perfect peace whose mind is stayed upon you for he trusteth in thee."

David—A Good Example of Faith & Fear

Ok. This is, what to me, is so mind boggling...powerful... David, after killing a nine foot six behemoth of a man, who Saul was afraid to deal with, within a few months David is now running from the very guy who had been running from the giant, saying these words;
 "I will one day perish at the hand of Saul. I better get out of here."
"I thought you'd killed the giant?"
"Yeah, but that was when I was in my prime."
"What do you mean that was in your prime?"
"Oh, I was thinking better in those days."

Let me try that again. I was thinking better those days. In those days, in my youth and in my young faith, I believed God for anything, but now I've learned to take care of myself. You know, God wants you to be a little rational, and a little reasonable, and...you know how it is. And by the way, when you get into that kind of slop, new people just kind of bug you, because they look like an image of you fifteen years ago. When they say, "God can do anything." And you go, "Oh you just wait until you're up against this wall."

The Sin is Not in Being Afraid—It's Staying Afraid

Let me try it again. "What time I am afraid...." It's not sin to be afraid; it's stupidity to stay afraid! "What time I am afraid I will trust in thee."

How are you going to trust in God looking at the problem? You got to get your eyeball off of the problem and start trusting God! You can't look at two objects at the same time unless you got a long span. David runs away...why?

His thoughts are tormenting him. Fear hath torment. Fear, therefore, having torment. Torment then produces actions accordingly. What does he do? He runs away.

We have people in this city who don't go to church anymore. You know why? They ran away. That's what Elijah did. Elijah ended a three and a half year drought with one prayer meeting. One prayer meeting! ...Kills four hundred and fifty prophets and outruns that ignorant Ahab's chariot ...gets one note from that old bag Jezebel, and he gets that thought in his head... "This chick's going to bump me off. I'm going to head for the wilderness."

Wait a minute. He just killed four hundred and fifty prophets. Brought fire down...brought water down...hand of the Lord on him...outruns the chariot.... All he gets is this dumb note from this floozy and he gets it and he reads it, "I'm going to kill you about this time of day tomorrow...turning you into a crispy critter...I'm going to cut your throat out and bar-b-que your hide. Love, Jezzy."

When Fear Grips, Run—To The Throne

Now let me finish. You need to understand why it so impacted him. Here's why. One, he's physically exhausted. Two, he's spiritually drained. And at that time comes this big, bad dude that hates your guts. He knows Jezebel didn't do anything about Mt. Carmel, and she knew what was going on at Mt. Carmel, because four hundred of her prophets were there, too. But Elijah was strong and his mind was clicking and he's walking like a caged tiger among these eight hundred and fifty fakers. He's mocking them and laughing. But after he's expended that spiritual juice and that physical frame is exhausted, now all of a sudden Jezebel comes and says, "Lets fight." And what happens? Instead of giving birth to faith, his thoughts go, "Oh God I just don't feel up to this." And fear says what? "If you don't feel up to it, run away to fight again. Go get some strength and R & R."

I'm telling you the truth. We have all experienced fear. We have all felt it. But we are not supposed to let it dominate us. What we are supposed to do, according to this Bible, is take fear to the throne. When we take fear to the throne, it then becomes an act of faith, which then pleases God. Truth sets you free. The Son makes you free. The captives are supposed to be set free. There are many things that cause fear.

Fear. It's the tormenter. Things that are causing fear are ignorance, sickness, the unknown, guilt and sin. The early church continued Jesus' ministry. They cast out spirits, they cleansed souls and they healed bodies. How? They declared Jesus.

It was Paul who was able to minister salvation to the Philippian jailer who arrived full of fear, but after truth was preached to him, traded fear for faith and got saved. Why? Because if Jesus sets you free you're free indeed.

Faith—The Antidote For Fear

Faith is the antidote for fear. And faith comes from the Word. James said, "Receive with meekness the ingrafted Word, which is able to save your souls." Ok, God wants us free in every area of our lives. If you're afraid then you're tormented. I don't care if you have your hair piled to the ceiling and your dress taped to your ankle...I don't care about that.

My God, you got a bunch of Hell inside you breaking loose and tormenting the dickens out of you like cancer eating somebody's life away. And that has got to come out of us.

The Bible says, "Perfect love casteth out *fear*." God's not given us a spirit of fear. I told you it was a spirit, and God's not given us a spirit of fear, but a sound mind. Why does He bring the spirit of *fear* in? And say sound mind? Well, because what Jeffery Wayne told you, "That stuff comes from here in your head!"

Chapter Two

Luke 1:67 "And his father Zacharias was filled with the Holy Ghost and prophesied, saying," ...In fact, I think I'll just handle that while I'm here.

The Holy Ghost—Old Testament vs. New Testament

Don't believe anybody that tells you that this fellow was baptized with the Holy Ghost. That's not the truth. That's not what this is saying. There are people who say, "Well, people had the Holy Ghost before the Holy Ghost was poured out." That's as dumb as it sounds. When it says, "He was filled with the Holy Ghost," it means *for function*; that the spirit of God moved on this man and in this man. Just like the Bible said, "The spirit was in prophets when they prophesied." But this was not a residency of the Holy Ghost that gave a new nature. There's a difference. Just like the Holy Ghost moved on Sampson for function. It was an anointing that gave power.

This is not the same as what happened at the day of Pentecost when the Holy Ghost took residency in people's spirit and they were born again. 'Cause if that is the case, then every time the Holy Ghost moved on these people, they were born again. This did not change their nature; this was only for function. The spirit came on 'em, they uttered, they moved, they displayed supernatural things...the spirit moved back again. But when you get the Holy Ghost, it moves in, it don't plan on moving out unless you kick it out. It's the truth!

What's Been Promised Must be Performed

Okay, let me try it again. "…And his father Zacharias was filled with the Holy Ghost, and prophesied, saying, Blessed be the Lord God of Israel; for he hath visited and redeemed his people…," now this is the Holy Ghost using this man. "…and hath raised up an horn of salvation for us in the house of his servant David; as he spake by the mouth of his holy prophets, which have been since the world began: That we should be saved from our enemies, and from the hand of all that hate us; to perform the mercy promised to our fathers."

Folks, things that are promised don't profit, unless they're performed. You can't live on the hopes and dreams and aspirations. You can't just say, "Well, someday it's going to happen." There's got to be a performance of what has been promised. And while you live in faith until that time happens, that period of time isn't your strength.

Performance Then Brings Fulfillment

It's when it's performed that you finally get a fulfillment of what you've been hoping and praying for. And so this spirit of God is telling this fellow to perform the mercy promised to our fathers, and to remember his holy covenant. The oath which he sware to our father Abraham, that he would grant unto us, that we being delivered out of the hand of our enemies might serve him without fear, in holiness and righteousness before him, all the days of our life.

"…and thou, child, shalt be called the prophet of the Highest: for thou shalt go before the face of the Lord to prepare his ways: To give knowledge of salvation unto his people by the remission of their sins, Through the tender mercy of our God; whereby the dayspring from on high hath visited us, To give light to them that sit in darkness and in the shadow of death," now watch this, "to guide our feet into the way of peace." That is the desire of God for his people...that we might walk in the way of peace...that we do not have inner turmoil.

John 8:32 "And ye shall know the truth, and the truth shall make you free."

Fear is an Alien Emotion

Fear. Last lesson, we showed you that fear was the first negative emotion that Adam had ever experienced. Until he trespassed the will and purpose of God, he never knew what fear was. Fear, if I understand this Bible, is an alien emotion. It was never the will of God for any human being to taste of. Just like sickness, sorrow, and death are all alien things that should never have come to us. God never intended for those to come to us. And to prove that God doesn't want 'em to come to us; when he removes the curse from our bodies, our spirits and this earth and the atmosphere, they will never come to us again.

So the perfect state is the absence of those things. Now, until we get to perfection where there's a totality and a completeness of the absence of those things, this Bible tells us God still wants us to taste the earnest of those things, and to be able to enjoy certain factors. There's one factor you'll never be able to enjoy until the rapture; and that's a new body.

But you do have an earnest of the Spirit in your spirit. You've tasted of the powers of the world to come. You do have a sensation of supernatural life in you when God gives you the Holy Ghost. That's why I'm so adamant that it's the will of God for you and me to be well, physically, because while the Holy Ghost is the earnest of our inheritance, than healing must also be the earnest of our inheritance, because we're going to have a totality of spirit at that day. And we're also going to have a totality of a new body at that day. So if we can taste of the earnest in the spirit, we oughta be able to taste of the earnest of a new body now.

Actions That Violate Revealed Will Produce Guilt and Guilt Brings Fear

Now, this man tasted fear. Where did the fear come from? It came from his thoughts. Thoughts effect emotion. The thoughts were negative. Fear was birthed, because it came directly from actions that were violating revealed will, and that produced guilt in him. And guilt will make you taste deep of fear.

If you have guilt, you naturally have the child of guilt, which is fear. Wait a minute; the other side. If you have righteousness, or innocence, you have no guilt—you have no fear. We are to serve the Lord without fear. And the best way to serve God without fear is to have a right relationship with God. If you have a right relationship, there is no fear.

We become afraid, because we either know something, or we don't know something. Therefore, fear was produced by violated knowledge. Trespass can produce fear. Therefore, obedience can produce peace. If I comply with what is revealed—here's where we miss it sometimes—I ain't gots to feel nothing. I have a peace that is born from knowledge that obeys. God wouldn't graduate us from emotionally realm-living, 'cause all of us at times say: "Well, I wonder if the Lord loves me?" How stupid that is! "Well, I wonder if I still got the Holy Ghost?" That's stupid!

God is Not a Tyrant

What do you think; that God is some nasty tyrant playing mystery games on you or something? ...Saying, "Well, I think I'll move in today...I'll move out tomorrow...Bet you can't find me...ha-ha-ha." That is so dumb! "Well he loved me yesterday, but I said a bad word today. Oh well, I'm going to hell."

And your child: you loved him or her yesterday and they did pretty good, but today they blew up the bathroom and they shot three dogs and they burned down your barn. Now you've just all of a sudden disinherited 'em, threw 'em out and sent 'em to jail. Oh, nice parent you are! Now, you may be angry; you may chastise them; you may say to them, "I'm very disappointed with you." But you certainly don't say to them, "You're disinherited—you broke the dishes.

Faith, Not Emotions, Says God Loves Us

Now, there are special times in all of our lives that it's neat, if I can use that word; neat, or cool, or nice, to feel the embrace of the love of God. And there are times when God does a special something; He just seems to come by your heart and goes, "I love you." And, boy, it just seems to refresh you and all the dry spell is gone and you go, "Oh, I'm saved again."

Well, you were saved ten minutes before He grabbed you, but it is just a nice thing to be embraced by the love of God, but God would have us to live on facts, because facts can do great battle with your feelings. But if you live by your emotions, your feelings will torment you. Take it from a man who knows. I read it somewhere...I'm going to show you how trespass and violated knowledge can produce fear.

Trespass & Violated Knowledge Produce Fear

Daniel 5:4 "They drank wine and praised the gods of gold, and of silver, of brass, of iron, of wood, and of stone. In the same hour came forth fingers of a man's hand, and wrote over against the candlestick upon the plaster of the wall of the king's palace: and the king saw the part of the hand that wrote. Then the king's countenance was changed, and his thoughts troubled him."

Ah, ha! Why did his thoughts trouble him? One, he knew better. Two, he doesn't understand what's being written. An ignorance of certain facts brings fear, and a demonstration of the supernatural, when you are carnal, brings fear. "...so that the joints of his loins were loosed."

My God, do you know what that means? There's a whole lot of shakin' going on. ...The joints of his loins...that's where his legs are attached. He's shakin', he ain't going to quit, man, he's shakin', and he's scared. I don't know if you've ever been that scared, but I've been scared enough that my legs felt like spaghetti. You ever felt like that? You got so terrified that you just were shakin', your mouth got dry and you just kinda....

Just think how you would react if all of a sudden a big hand just walked into your building...just started writing. Scared him half to death. But he knew he shouldn't have done what he'd done. It was bad enough that he was having a drunken orgy. To go and violate Gods honor and his purity and take the vessels that were dedicated to Jehovah and start praising the Gods of gold and silver with the vessels dedicated to God...that tells me something. We are the vessels of the Lord.

Misuse of God's Vessel (Our Body) is a Trespass

It is absolute trespass, and does violence and reproach to the holiness of God to take the vessels of the Lord and praise the Gods of this world, or the Gods of silver and gold, wine, drink, or whatever. If God didn't take that lightly, and they were just pieces of ornamentation that were dedicated to the use of the service of the temple, how much more, when we are the temples of the living God, that we should be very, very careful what we should let our bodies get involved in.

And that goes over real bad in our day with a lot of people who are always preaching this liberty foolishness. But we are the temples of the Lord and we need to be very careful *what* we use our bodies to praise.

Verse 9 "The king cried aloud to bring in the astrologers, the Chaldeans and the soothsayers. And the king spake, and said to the wise men of Babylon, Whosoever shall read this writing, and shew me the interpretation thereof, shall be clothed with scarlet, and have a chain of gold about his neck, and shall be the third ruler in the kingdom."

People Need Relief—Not Rules

Now, there's a principal being revealed here, folks. There is, at the heart of men and women, such a yearning and deep desire to get relief when they are afraid. And he's asking, "Anybody that can get me some relief, I'll reward you." Now, he's doing it for the wrong thing, because he don't want to get right with God. But there are people who are coming among us, who are also saying, in their anguished look and their feeling, "I need relief!" "I'll do anything to get relief." "I'll give anything to get relief."

If we can create an atmosphere that the King of Glory can give people relief from their fears, they will find it very easy to give of themselves to Him that gives relief. What people need, folks, is relief, not rules. Relief! Because if you can give somebody relief and then speak to them from the same throne that gave relief and say, "The one that gave you relief would like you to do this...." they'd jump on and say, "Fine!" But, if you ask them to do it and they still don't have relief, now they're frustrated.

Fear is Produced in Many Ways

"...Then came in all the king's wise men: but they could not read the writing, nor make known to the king the interpretation thereof. Then was king Belshazzar greatly troubled."

Now he's more afraid, and his countenance was changed in him. Everybody's shook up. Fear is produced by guilt. Now, I'm gonna get this to you: Fear...it's not the only way...don't say, "Oh my, I'm guilty, because I'm afraid." No, no. That's one of the multiple ways that fear is produced; there's guilt, trespass, transgression. The Bible says, "The sinners in Zion are greatly afraid." Rightly so.

In the end time, the Bible talks about the end-time wrath in Revelation 6:15-17. The Bible says, "They cried out to kings and the rulers of the earth said, let the rocks and stones fall on us and let them hide us from the face of him that one sitteth on the throne, and from the wrath of the lamb:" Why? They knew better! They cursed God. They'd done stuff that God told them not to do.

Now, all of sudden God says, "Okay, it's payday pal." And they're saying, "Let them mountains fall on us, let the rocks...." Don't think sinners are winning. They may laugh at you, and stick their tongue out, and say you're living in a prison camp. You just wait until Revelation 6 comes. God doesn't pay off in the first month of harvest. I wouldn't be in that crew for all the tea in China. To be running away from the wrath of Him that sits on the throne, saying, "Oh, I could've been saved, but I was a jerk." Notice, nobody was running to a square dance and looking for a bottle of whiskey. They were looking to run and hide. The very thing people can't give up to serve God, they're going to give up when they get to the lake of fire.

Fear is Produced When we Violate Knowledge

Consider, ladies and gentlemen, times that you and I have been afraid of our parents...come on; swallow hard now. Mom and Dad said do this and do that, or don't do this, or don't do that. We did it. We all fudged corners. We all cut corners. We try...you know.

Mom and Dad were never children; they were born 43. They've never done the things we've done; they were always old. And all of a sudden Dad and Mom's comin' home, and you were supposed to do this thing and do that thing...all of a sudden you have this great sensation inside you. This tingly-somethin'. And when they walk in they say;
"Hey, Jeffrey. How are you?"
"Hi, fine...."
"Are you glad to see me?"
"Oh, man I'm so thrilled you're here."

What's happened? ...Violated knowledge. And usually most parents, when they got ready to correct you, turned around and said, "Didn't I tell you?" And they make you go over the whole thing before they give you a good shot, or they punish you. You're afraid...and then you tingle again...different area.

Fear used to be produced in my life as a kid from my, from my...I don't want to say lousy, 'cause the guy's dead...my brother. 'Cause he used to have a terrible thing he used to do to me. He'd always say, "I'm going to tell!" And he'd ruin my whole day, because he would release in me this negative factor. He didn't mind getting whipped, I don't know why. He'd take a whuppin' and get me a whuppin'. And Mom said I'd have to do this and do that, and I didn't want to do it. And so I wouldn't do it and we'd fight and carry on all day, and then when my mom and dad was coming home Bruce would just say, "I'm telling!" And that thing just ate on me all day long, 'cause I knew that if he told, I'm in trouble. And I'm in trouble 'cause I knew better.

Criminals fear the police...the judge. Why? Because they violated knowledge. Now, I'm going to get a little closer to us. Writing predated checks produces in us sometimes a feeling, "...I hope he doesn't cash it before it clears." Not much response now. It's always a humorous thing for someone to hand me a check and say;
"Here you go, don't cash that."
"Say, why did you write it?"
"Well, I just wanted you to think you got paid."

Now, all of us at times have run very close on funds, or shy on funds, ...don't raise your hands please; and you know what I'm talking about; that sometimes you've cut it so close that you don't know whether you're over five bucks, or short ten dollars or something; and in your heart you're going...thump, thump, thump. And you get that little notice from the bank, and the minute you see it you go, "Ohhh." And there's that fear that comes from violating knowledge 'cause you know you shouldn't do that, but you were hoping that it would take two more days to clear than it did. Your intentions were pure…, "I'll have the money in there Friday." "If he doesn't cash that check until Friday, we're home safe." But for three days you're having torment, because the Bible says, "Fear bringeth torment."

Have you ever driven your car and didn't have your brakes working right? And you drive down the street on a wing-and-a-prayer. I drove a car one time…only had one set of shoes working; the right front. I was just a young kid…they were *all* safe to me! When you get a little older you don't do stuff like that. Or you drive down the street and you know your tag's expired, but you hope there's no police. Or you leave your wallet at home, or you don't *have* a drivers license. Now, you might get by…you're hoping to get by, but all the while…while you're doing it, there is, in the pit of your stomach, FEAR! Why? Because trespass gives birth to fear.

The Only Work of Fear is Torment

When you violate knowledge, even if it's major or minor, it's fear. And the only work of fear is torment. Don't blame *fear*; it's doing a great job! That's what it was birthed to do, create torment! You oughta turn and congratulate it, "Thanks fear, you're never sitting down on the job!" "You're always doin' your job full-fledged, you're always creatin' a lousy day for me." Yet, if you do what you're supposed to do, that obedience produces such a tranquility and such a confidence and such a peace. You would think that because we enjoy peace and tranquility so much that we would always try to do that.

There's something in the human species, somewhere here in this hole, that somehow says, "Not me. I will not get caught." I've said this…you've never said this…I've said this: "God will watch out for me, for I pay my tithes." As the little bubble gum machine goes around...say's, "We're not in the tithes business, we're in the ticket business." I am hitting a home run tonight! We all have this funny feeling in our stomach..., "I hope we don't get caught."

Faith—The Archenemy of Fear

Faith is the antidote for fear, but faith comes to us from the Word of God. Now, it's not enough to tell you what fear does and how it comes to ya, I need to try to help you get rid of it: Faith comes from the Word of God. And *faith* is the archenemy of *fear*, because faith in God will produce tranquility, and fear will produce torment. When we *receive*, James said, "With meekness the ingrafted word it is able to save our souls."

God Delivers Us From Fear—Not Always the Situation

In Psalms 34:4 David says, "I sought the Lord, and he heard me, and delivered me from all my fears." All my fears! I'm going to say something right now that you've probably never heard, but it's the truth anyway: God can and does deliver you from your fears without delivering you from your situation. And a lot of times we think it's the situation that's produced the fear. Oh no it isn't! God will let you stay in the situation and you still don't have to have any fear. Why? "Because I sought the Lord and he heard me, and delivered me from my *situation?*" No; from my *fears*.

We're always, all of us, trying to get away from the situation. When you can stay in the situation, but if you would have a right relationship with God and a balance with the Book, you can stay in that situation and not be tormented by fear, because when you seek God, that's an act of *faith*.

Watch this; this is heavy stuff here; Psalm 56:1, "Be merciful unto me, O God: for man would swallow me up; he fighting daily oppresseth me. Mine enemies would daily swallow me up: for they be many that fight against me, O thou most High."

Now, this is a powerful statement David makes. Watch; "What time I am afraid, I will trust in thee." That's impossible to do, unless you release *faith*. "…What time I am afraid," literally, when I am afraid, I'm going to trust in You. That means fear is giving you the dickens, it's causing you torment and turmoil and in the midst of that scenario, you say, "I know You're good and I know You're wonderful. I'm taking my fear to the throne." And when you take your fear to the throne, that's an act of faith and that pleases God. Well, I'm telling you the truth anyway.

Changing Location Doesn't Dispel Fear Because Every Where You Go, There You Are

"In God I will praise his Word, in God I have put my trust; I will not fear what flesh can do unto me." This is written by a man that knows all about fear, because he ran away from situations. He got tired of Saul chasing him, what did he do? He changed geography. But you change geography…the same spirit of fear goes with you.

"Now, if I can just get out from underneath that problem, I'll be okay." And it looked like for, a while, that he had the answer, 'cause the minute he got out of the reach of Saul and went down to the Philistine land, Saul wasn't bugging him anymore. But the same problem was there. The problem wasn't solved; the problem was David.

And one day he comes home and Ziklag is like an ashtray. It's burnt to the ground. His wife is gone, his children are gone and now the people that were following him are now going to kill him. So, he did what he said, "in the midst of my fear, I called on the Lord. I went to you, what time I am afraid, I will trust in thee." Honey, it's hard to trust when you're afraid, unless you can release faith. That's the great battle.

See, most of us...be honest...most of us have the mentality of the situation. You're in this cruddy, lousy situation, so we just say, "Abort!" "Now I won't have any problems." Watch: "My problem's over here. But if I would stand here, in the situation that's causing me terror and trial and trouble and problem and say, 'What time I am afraid, I will trust in thee, I will look in your direction, I'll call on you and you'll deliver me out of my fears. I don't need to leave the situation.'"

Take Fear to the Throne

God may allow us to stay in the situation. To seek God when we are afraid is a great act of *faith*. To take fear to the throne pleases God. Hebrews 11:6, "He that cometh to God must believe that he is, and that he is a rewarder of them that diligently seek him." He said he'd deliver me from all my fears. Why? He rewards those that diligently seek him.

I really believe this folks. In all of our lives, mine especially, we are so situation-oriented, rather than Savior oriented. "...Well, if I can just get out of this situation...." I know that there are some situations that are not conducive. That if God will lead you, you need to get out of it, but it seems like everyday of our lives, we're always stealing away from situations. We're almost like...wanting to build a convent to live in it. "...What time I am afraid, I will trust in thee. 'And if I can trust in you....'"

I told you, God will not take us out of some situations. He may leave us stay there, but he will not let us be tormented by fear. Point in case: Daniel in the lion's den.... He didn't take Daniel out of the den. He gave Daniel a good night's sleep. Now, if I had been there, I'd say, "Kill these lions! Quick!!" Go ahead and laugh. ...as if you wouldn't. I'd be standing over in the corner saying, "In Jesus name...!" But Daniel...he just goes out, looks at these lions and, watch; he's in a terrible situation, a death situation. Yet he says, "What time I am afraid, I will trust in thee." And when he looks towards God and trusts in God, God is pleased with an act of faith. He goes back and just puts a spirit of sleep on the lions and ol' Daniel just kinda pushes up and says, "Get over there a little bit, I need a pillow." Hey, read the story! The only guy that didn't sleep was the king that sent him there. The king stayed awake all night. Daniel's snoring!
"Ain't you afraid?"
"Yea, I was afraid."
"What'd you do with your fears?"
"Took em to the throne!"

God Gives Peace in the Situation

Come on, let it sink. God won't take you sometimes out of the situation, He'll just give you peace in the situation. Why? If you take your fear to the throne.

Simon Peter's put in jail and he's between a bunch of soldiers and he's chained to the wall and they got him in the inner prison. And they're going to take his head off the next day. What's he do? Sleeps. "What would you do?" "Talk in tongues all night." "I'd pray, really get a hold of God." What? Why don't you just go lay down?"

What makes Peter go to sleep? Watch! Knowledge of truth attacks the thing that can breed fear. He looks at his death sentence. Come on, there's no way he can get out. He ain't gonna kung fu everybody, ain't no way he can get out. So, what does he do? He thinks. Why? Because thought produces fear, or tranquility. And he thinks... "Now, what am I doing in this situation? What's going to happen to me?" And he just goes back to sleep.
"I don't know if you do that, but I got a catalog in my head, it goes way back many years. Just got little topics in it and I just kind of go back. Okay...insert back...use it later."

And one came out of his brain, it says, "Print it up on the screen: 'When thou art old, another will bind thee and take thee where they don't want to go.'" And he made the sign of the cross to show 'em how he'd glorify Him. And he goes... "I'm supposed to get crucified. Herod's fixin' to behead me. I'm going to sleep." See what delivers you from fear? The knowledge of the Holy.

Who Gives the Spirit of Fear?

Okay, the Bible says, "Fear hath torment." II Timothy 1:7; "For God hath not given us the spirit of fear." Well then, if God hasn't given us the spirit of fear, I want to know who gave it to us. If we say as one of these fellows said tonight, "There ain't but two forces in the world, good and evil...God and the devil...if God didn't give me the spirit of fear, who gave me the spirit of fear?"

Who gives you the spirit of fear? If this man says, "God hath not given us the spirit of fear." "...but of power, and of love, and of a sound mind," because if you don't have a sound mind, you're going to have fear. God does not give us the spirit of fear.

Spirit of Fear Cast Out With Words

The Bible says, "Perfect love casteth out fear." Now, wait a minute. To cast out something doesn't do any good unless you replace it. You can take the word of God, cast out a spirit of fear and torment; you can just cast it out, you can speak to it. Spirits go out by words. You don't plead the blood against them; they go out by words..."Command you in Jesus name, come out!" ...they have to leave. They have to obey the word of...
"Oh, they don't obey me."
"Sure, they obey you."

You're not the authority, you're not the power. The Word's the power; he's subject to this Book. I don't care if you feel like you're a spiritual midget. That has nothing to do with it. If you are living righteous, pure, before God, and you have contact with God, whether you feel it or not, you have a righteous standing with God. You can quote this scripture and that spirit has to obey, but when you cast it out, you need to replace it with something. So, what does God do? He says, "God's not given us a spirit of fear." So, he replaces it with a spirit of power, and a spirit of love, and of a sound mind. That's what we've done in the Pentecostal ranks.

What's Been Cast Out Must be Replaced

We've preached against so much all the time.... We've taken eighty million things away from everybody and gave 'em back four. Now you've created a great canyon. Come on, there's a law of nature friend; that when you create a vacuum, something's going to come. You throw the tenants out of your house, "Get out of there you slobs." That's fine. You say, "Boy, I showed them." Nine months later your house is still empty. I got news for you, it ain't empty! Now you got mice, snakes, roaches, chameleons, spider webs, spiders, you got all kinds of little creepy creatures that will move in that vacant house for you, uninvited! You think that you can cast a spirit out of you of fear or torment, and then you don't replace it with something, and it's just gonna be a neat little vacuum? There's creeping things moving throughout this whole earth that are looking for a vacant spot.

Replace Fear With Things of God

Isaiah 26:3, "Thou wilt keep him in perfect peace, whose mind is stayed on thee: because he trusteth in thee." Get your mind on the things of God! Fill your mind with the promises of God, and fear will not be allowed to torment you. We are to replace fear's thoughts with the thoughts of God. You don't just cast out, you put back in. "What time I am afraid, I will trust in thee." Release from fear is the result of replacing it...not just emptying out, but filling back up. If you fill your mind and your heart with the words of God, fear is not allowed to bring you torment, because fear comes from thought, not just from trespass.

How many people ever think things that you didn't just "conjure up"? Ever wonder why you're walkin' down the street and all of a sudden you have a thought that makes you wonder where it came from? Have you ever been disillusioned with yourself and just disappointed with yourself and say, "What am I, a dirty old man?" Isaiah 54:14, "In righteousness shalt thou be established: thou shalt be far from oppression; for thou shalt not fear: and from terror; for it shall not come near thee." Why will you be far from oppression? Because you're not gonna be afraid. Why are you not gonna be afraid? Because you are established in righteousness.

No Fear—No Oppression

When we are established in righteousness, oppression is far away. Fear is the root of all oppression, but the Bible says that because we're established in righteousness, oppression shall be far away from you, because you don't have any fear. If you don't have any fear you can't be oppressed.

WE ARE the Righteousness of God

Jesus was made our righteousness. 2 Corinthians 5:17-19, 21, it says that we have become the righteousness of God in Him; our movement has never believed that as far as I know. I have never heard at General Conference, or camp meeting, or a Bible study, or sermon on "we are the righteousness of God." What are we afraid of? I just don't understand; now either God is lying, or He is telling the truth.

This Book says that when I am born again of water and Spirit, I become the righteousness of God in Him. Whether I feel dirty, stinky, lousy, guilty, or what, has nothing to do with it! This Book is the criteria for all things, and it says that we become the righteousness of God in Him!

When we are put in Him, and He is put in us, I'm righteous. You say, "Well, he makes mistakes." That has nothing to do with it. I'm righteous. I am in righteous standing before God, and if I have a righteous standing, torment and oppression and fear are not allowed to do anything with me; I have a righteous standing. But we react so much to misdeeds, to emotions, thoughts and feelings... as if they had the power to undo our righteous standing.

Here I am, a child of God, I've got the Holy Ghost, I'm baptized in Jesus name, I'm doing all that I know how to do. I live for God, I go through a low spell in my life…a bad season, I'm not praying much, I'm being kind of oppressed by things I'm allowing in my life, I'm getting critical, I murmur once in a while. I've opened the door to some spirits that have tormented the dickens out of me, and in a moment of weakness I do something stupid. Now I'm gonna be tormented from guilt, because I knew better. But I gotta say, 'now wait a minute God; I confess my sin, You are faithful and just to forgive.' You know what God does? I didn't get taken out of the body because I sinned, I'm in the body, but He let's the blood work on me so that I'm reestablished in my righteous standing.

Satan, The Accuser

But six weeks later the devil is sayin', 'You're done, you did it.' He's a lying dog, he's the one that's outside the body. I'm in the body. You know why he says that? Because he's not righteous, and never will be able to be righteous. He hates your guts, because you've got something he ain't got. He made one sin and God cast him out forever, …goin' to a lake of fire, won't let him repent, won't let him get baptized, won't let him get the Holy Ghost, won't let him get forgiven, but we can fail and we can make mistakes and we can go to the bloody throne and we can plead the benefits of the blessings of the blood, and because we're established in righteousness, oppression shall be far from us where we will not have any fear!!!

Peace With God

Because we're established in righteousness, oppression is far from us, therefore; Romans 5:1 comes to pass in our lives…"Being justified by faith, we have peace with God through our Lord Jesus Christ." Which means that I can have peace while all of Hell is trying to eat my lunch, and situations can be trying to suck me down into the sewer, but I have peace with God.

If you don't believe the Word, it's ineffective to you. You need to tell yourself, "Being justified by faith I have peace with God." You can have peace with God and not be doing everything to the letter. Sometimes we don't have peace, because we don't do everything everybody expects us to do.

The devil is the bum that's out there trying to play cop and put guilt on you. We can just go to the Judge. You are justified by faith, you're established in righteousness. You're not a dirty devil, you're a Son of God. You've got His nature, you've got His name, you've got His power. Don't pay attention to all that stuff; he couldn't tell the truth standing on a Bible looking at Jesus. He has been labeled forever a liar. Why believe it? Yet, every one of us, the best of us, the most spiritual of us, have believed him. He suggests something to us, and we go, "Oh, that's the truth." If you don't get it out of your head, you know what he does? He just puts it on the shelf, and then when you're not feeling well, when you're under pressure.... You know, he brings up things in my life, that me and God have both forgotten.

Ignorance, The Unexplained & Unknown Cause Fear

The devil's got a tremendous memory, especially when there's been a little irritation. There are other things that can produce fear in us: one is ignorance; one is the unexplained; the other is the unknown that can cause fear to rise. We react to things that we cannot grasp, that we're not able to catalog via reason and knowledge. If we know something, or we have experienced something, that knowledge or experience creates in us a comfortable relaxation. If we do not know, or we have not experienced, the immediate reaction is uneasiness, apprehension, even anxiety. That's why, sometimes, when visitors come to see us and we start jukin' and jumpin' and clappin' and talking in tongues, the visitor, they don't mean to, but this is uncharted water for them, and they look at us and wonder what is our problem. And we look at them and say, "What's the matter? Don't you love God?"

Yeah, they love God, but they're out here scuba diving' and they ain't never been in the water.... "I don't mind scuba diving in my bathtub, but I'm not much for going to the lagoon where the creature from the black lagoon lives. I'm real apprehensive about going around the moray eels and barracudas. I'm not comfortable with that."

So here is somebody walking in from out of a whole world of sin and they don't know anything about spiritual enterprise and they're just blown away by it, so they're uneasy. You know what we're supposed to do? Give 'em room. Create an atmosphere that they can be comfortable.

Jesus raised the dead, He healed the sick, He cleansed the lepers, He cast out spirits, and again and again and again it says these words, "and great fear fell upon them." That was not reverence; they were tormented with fear, because they didn't understand. Howbeit they were astonished with His doctrine, for His word was with power; He cast out spirits with His word. A boy with an epileptic seizure in Mark 9...falling on the ground, and Jesus said, "come out of him," and the boy was okay.

We Need the Word—Not Reason

Reason is an arrangement. To grasp this kind of stuff requires faith. Some people don't have faith, because they don't have any Word, all they have is reason. Reason rages when situations are beyond its ability. Faith is beyond reason, therefore; without faith, reason breeds fear, but if we use faith it brings to us calmness.

Point in case, in Mark 4 they were told; "let's go to the other side in the boat." The Bible says they get into a storm, they become afraid of the storm. Why? Because they don't know to what velocity the storm will get, and they also know that storms can capsize boats and kill people. So it's what they don't know and some of what they do know that's bringing fear to them, so they waken the Master and say, "Carest not that we perish?"

So they're afraid of the storm, they awaken Jesus, Jesus goes to the bow of the boat, Jesus is very relaxed and peaceful…released what was alive inside of Him into the situation that was outside of Him, and what was outside of Him became like what was inside.

Release What's Inside With Words

If He can release it with words, why can't we. When the situation is bringing fear to us, why don't we just speak what's inside of us alive and reduce the situation to become what's inside of us. So whether we're taken out of situation, or not, we can make fear leave.

The only problem these boys had is, once He released what was inside of Him, what was inside of Him now scared them. They turned around with great fear and said, "What manner of man is this that now He puts nature to sleep?"

There are people who are afraid of the supernatural. Why? Not because they're devils, or spiritual midgets, but because they don't understand. They haven't learned yet, they haven't experienced it.

Think for a moment...when you go to take a new job. Why do you have that *funny* feeling in your stomach? Because you're uncomfortable of the unknown of what is required of you. Sometimes, when you get involved with something that you are not experienced in, if you are not careful, you'll revert back to what's comfortable to you...but you don't make any progress.

Ever feel fear when you make a wrong turn and you get lost? You're just driving a dumb car on a dumb street and all of a sudden, after a mile, your wife tells ya, "This area has already been discovered, we don't have to go this way." After a while you're down in the dump somewhere and there's a *hood* standing there swingin' a chain sayin', "How ya doin? Glad you're donating your car." Fear comes from the unknown, uncharted.

Fear Breeds Unbelief

Our minds play games with us, our minds create images, our minds birth feelings, fear also breeds unbelief, which is revealed in words and actions, which finally result in divine displeasure. Israel saw the giants and were afraid. Joshua and Caleb saw God and were fearless; they were both in the same situation, one's afraid, one's full of faith. Why? "What time I am afraid, I will trust in thee." What was Joshua's and Caleb's statement, "the Lord who has delivered us from all this, surely He will be with us now." They looked back in their past and said, "He's never failed us, what's the big deal, He took us out of Egypt, He rolled back the Red Sea, He's the miracle God, come on, they're bread for us, let's go."

You Gotta Learn to Fight

In order to release faith, you release human will. You must fight your fear and some of you right now are tormented by fear, not because you're spiritual jerks, or little babies, not so, it's because you have not been taught to fight! You think those of us that live some type of measure of a victorious life are some kind of spiritual giants? We are not! We are people who just say, "No, I'm gonna fight the good fight of faith." "I'm gonna lay hold of eternal life." "I'm not gonna let this thing torment me." "I'm not a dog to let this thing jerk at my neck." "I've got righteousness, I've got holiness, I've got power, and I've got authority." "It doesn't matter what I feel, what time I am afraid I will trust in thee." You gotta do it!

You've got the Holy Ghost, you're not supposed to live in fear and anxiety and torment. You're not! God is real, and the Word of God is real. You are greatly loved by God, and God does not want you to be tormented, but to have peace. It's not just gonna come to you, it's not gonna happen just because you quote scripture. You gotta fight! If you don't battle, you lose! Everything in nature that ceases to struggle, ceases. How much more everything in the spiritual realm that ceases to struggle ceases to live?

The Things of God Are Spiritually Discerned

What about Jesus when He went to the Gadarenes? He cast the devils out of that man and what happened? Did He get any response? Yeah, two! The fella He cast the devil out of said, "Boy this is great, swell, wonderful." The other crew said, "Get outta here." Why? They were afraid.

Why? Because they couldn't understand it. They couldn't catalog the supernatural, had never seen it happen before.

"The natural man receiveth not the things of God for they are spiritually discerned." So you say, "Well this guy was a natural man." Yeah, well, wait, but he experienced something. The natural man can experience the supernatural and not be able to understand it, or equate it to anything he's had in his life, but can say, "I don't know how it worked, all I know is it worked."

Why Speaking in Tongues is Rejected by Many

Why does the world reject speaking in tongues as evidence of the Holy Ghost? Because it requires of the natural man to step from that plateau to the supernatural; which is now uncomfortable, because they've never worked there before. They've had a twenty-year existence in this nice little carnal, intellectual, reasonable, comfortable area, and here comes you characters sayin', "Ya need the Holy Ghost talkin' in tongues!" That makes somebody uncomfortable, uneasy, and unless they're honest, they won't react, they'll reject.

Satan's Greatest Tool—Fear—From Seeing Pictures in Your Mind and Feeling Them

Fear is Satan's greatest tool; people reject Jesus Christ over fear. They imagine the wrong things about Jesus and the church. They see things in their mind, first. Fear is not only something you feel, it's something you see. You ever describe something to somebody and they go, "Oh, I see." A thought makes images, pictures.

The thoughts that we have, end up drawing pictures in our mind. After you've drawn a picture in your mind, you can

begin to feel the picture. Create an image in your mind and you can literally feel the picture. You see something you are afraid of and you feel fear. Something you're anxious over, all of a sudden you can feel it, it becomes very real. In the parable of the talents, the man's confession that damned him forever was these words...
"I was afraid."
"Sir, what made you afraid?"
"I pictured in my mind you were a hard man."
"Where did you get that thought? ...A lie from the devil! He created that thought in your mind. You made a picture of it and you recorded it."

And from that time on you viewed him as a hard man. Therefore, you hid your talent. You can actually feel what you begin to see. That's why when you get an image of Jesus Christ and He's beautiful, you can feel that warmth, the excellency, that vibrancy. You can feel Him.

Revelation 21:8, the thing that leads the whole list of the unbelieving, the abominable, murderers, whoremongers, sorcerers, idolaters, all liars is but the fearful. They go to hell first. Why? Because fear is the archenemy of faith. Only faith pleases God.

Overcome Fear With Knowledge & Experience

Fear is the greatest hindrance to our walk, yet God cries out, "Fear not, it's your Father's good pleasure to give you the kingdom!" So how do we overcome fear? Knowledge and experience. "What time I am afraid I will trust in thee." Take the Word of God and create a picture in your mind. "In God I put my trust and will not be afraid what man can do to me, for thou hast delivered my soul from death, wilt thou not deliver my feet from falling, that I may walk before God in the light of the living."

Psalm 27:1 "The Lord is my light and my salvation: whom shall I fear? The Lord is the strength of my life; of whom shall I be afraid?" ...David's got a picture in his mind. Without the picture of the Lord in your mind fear is gonna torment you. So David starts out with, "The Lord is my light and the Lord is my strength, and the Lord is my security, what am I gonna be afraid of?"

2: "When the wicked, even my enemies and my foes, came upon me to eat up my flesh, they stumbled and fell."

3: "Though an host should encamp against me, my heart shall not fear: though war should rise against me, in this will I be confident."

5: "For in the time of trouble he shall hide me in his pavilion: in the secret of his tabernacle shall he hide me; he shall set me up upon a rock.

6: "And now shall mine head be lifted up above mine enemies round about me: therefore will I offer in his tabernacle sacrifices of joy; I will sing, yea, I will sing praises unto the Lord. Amen."

Destroy the Seed Before it Takes Root

Your homework assignment is Isaiah 41:10-14, it repeats "do not be afraid, do not be afraid. I the Lord will hold your hand, I will keep you, I will not let the devourer get you. Do not be afraid I will hold you, I will deliver you, Israel."

It even says, "O Jacob, thou worm, be not afraid I'll keep thee, I'll hold thee, I'll grab thee by the hand." What's He trying to get people to do? Release their faith! You gotta deal with the seed. The devil will drop a seed in your mind. You need the Word of God as an axe to dig it up and cut it out. Take it out by the root, so you won't have any fruit of what the devil planted in your mind.

Chapter Three

Faith Only Comes From God's Word

Psalm 27:1, "The Lord is my light and my salvation; whom shall I fear? The Lord is the strength of my life; of whom shall I be afraid?"

David, that is a mouthful. Something tells me that what David just said didn't always work in David's life. You can name it and claim it, you can quote it and do all you want to, but there are times when you are just low. There are times when you are under the gun. There are times when you seem like you can't hardly muster just a childlike faith. And there are times when you grab a hold of it and say, "Boy I just feel like I could run through a troop and leap over a wall." There are! And there are other times you will say, "I was running towards that wall and it fell on me." Then you kind of scramble out of the rubble.

Verse2, "When the wicked, even mine enemies and my foes, came upon me to eat up my flesh, they stumbled and fell."

That is a powerful scripture. Do you know what the enemy was? You know, we look at this and say, "Yeah, some dudes that didn't like David." You know what? His enemy was also sickness. Sickness is no friend of the Child of God. And it says, "When my enemies come up...." To do what? "Eat up my flesh...." What does sickness do? "When the wicked, even mine enemies and my foes, came upon me to eat up my flesh, they stumbled and fell." What makes sickness stumble and fall...? Because you've got confidence in God who is your light and your life and you refuse to be afraid, there is only one thing that can stop fear from rampaging, and that is faith. And you only get faith from God's Word.

Verse 3, "Though an host should encamp against me, my heart shall not fear;" Now that seems like a total contradiction. How could you be encamped around on all sides with all kinds of situations beating in your head and yet you say, "Ah, my heart is not going to be afraid of what I see. My heart is not going to be afraid of what I hear." Why, David? Watch what he says; "Though war should rise against me, in this will I be confident."

Confidence in the Lord Being Your Light & Life

In what? What does he mean, "in this?" In Verse 1, he is stating this; why are you not going to be afraid? "'Cause the Lord is my light and the life of my salvation. He is my salvation, whom shall I fear? The Lord is the strength of my life, who am I going to be afraid of?" Then he tells you; the camp is around about you, I am not going to be afraid. "In this will I be confident." In what? In Verse 1, that "the Lord is the light." ...He's my light; I'm not going to be afraid of what people try to do to me, of what sickness will try to do to me, what devils will try to do to me. Why? "'Cause the Lord is my light." Do you get it?

Okay, let's go a little further, Psalm 34:1-6. Apparently, you know by now I am going to be talking about fear. "...I will bless the Lord at all times..." Tough to do! You know folks, some of the greatest decisions you make is not between right and wrong, it is between right and right. You just chew on that a little while.

..."His praise shall continually be in my mouth." But sometimes all I have is praise in my mouth...I have lockjaw.... It's in the fine print right here.

(2) "My soul shall make her boast in the Lord…" How can a man or a woman's soul boast in the Lord, lest his mouth opens?
…"The humble shall hear thereof, and be glad." The haughty will get bent out of shape.
(3) "O magnify the Lord with me, and let us exalt his name together."
(4) "I sought the Lord, and he heard me, and delivered me from all my fears."

That is an act of faith when you are afraid and you go to the throne and say, "I'm afraid, but I am here in faith, anyway." That pleases God. That is why the writer in Hebrews 11 said, "Now God is a rewarder of them that diligently seek him. For without faith it is impossible to please him." So when you are afraid and you still go to the throne in an act of faith, that pleases God, and when people enter that dimension where you are pleasing God, God will reward you.

Fear, Worry & Anxiousness—The Three Faced Evil

That is what David said, "I sought the Lord and he delivered me—the reward—from all my fears." I am telling you my friend, it is better to be delivered from fear than any other problem, because fear gives birth to everything that is negative. That is why the writer said, "Fear hath torment." Fear has a twin sister named Worry and he has an ugly brother named Anxiousness. Boy, when you get that trinity in your house, you've got problems. It will take one God to cast out that devil.
(5) "They looked unto him and were lightened: and their faces were not ashamed."
(6) "This poor man cried, and the Lord heard him, and saved him out of all his troubles."

Psalm 56:1-3, "Be merciful unto me, O God: for man would swallow me up; he fighting daily oppresseth me."
(2) Mine enemies would daily swallow me up: for they be many that fight against me, O thou most High."
(3) "What time I am afraid, I will trust in Thee."
So many of us at times in our lives have said, "Boy if I just wasn't so anxious and so fretful and so fearful, I could just somehow get close to God." "I would do better." "Oh, if I could just...if I could just get from this fear, I could worship."

He said, "What time I am afraid, while I am experiencing the fear, I will turn my face towards Him and trust in Him." Now that is a tremendous demonstration of faith. When you are afraid and you force your flesh to say, "I will not be afraid." "You are good to me." "I trust you." "I love you." "It will be ok....."

Fear—The First Negative Emotion in Mankind

We have studied, the last couple of chapters, that fear can come from trespass. When we have a revealed will of God given to us such as Adam and Eve had in the garden...they were told not to eat the fruit of that tree. They willingly trespassed, and from that they received guilt. Guilt of violated law or understood law will produce fear in you. It was the first emotion that they ever felt. That is why fear is a hard thing to battle with. It is the oldest negative emotion that the human race has ever tasted. It was *the first* negative emotion.

You can sit there and act real stone faced like, "I am never afraid." You are lying. Whether you have anxiety attacks, whether you eat your fingernails to the elbows, whether you get sweaty palms, or whether you get butterflies in your belly; everybody feels this thing called fear. It is very, very real. And in some people, it is more tormenting than in others. I have to believe that God has dealt with me about this the last month or so, because God wants you and I free from it. While we so long emphasize, as Pentecostal holy rollers, *a good Sunday night is like a good drug shot*. If you can just get a good Sunday night of banging the walls and talking in tongues a little bit...whoa...you've got it! We've learned after 30 years of frustrated people that Sunday fizzles before Monday morning is here. And the rage of your emotions goes up and down before Wednesday is here.

"It Is Written"—Not All You Need

So the thing that will help us is Biblical knowledge. You have to have in you, just like Jesus did, "It is written..." "It is written... "It is written..." You have got to, because Jesus' emotion wasn't high in the wilderness when he met the devil. It was low. He was lonely. He was out of gas. He was 40 days fasting. He was weak physically. His mind was there...he was fixing to enter a brand new journey...he was going to be the only one who ever believed what he was going to preach...he was there all alone and here comes this thing and it appeals to every area of his being...and he has got to be able to say, "It is written...."

I am going to tell you, just because you say, "It is written...," don't expect the devil to say, "Oh wow, let me just run away." Friend, you slam one door, he just opens another. After a while when he realizes that you know what the Book says, he will depart from you for a season. Then he'll come back in another attack. That is why you need to know the Book better than you know television. I am serious about that.

We Need the Power of the Author

We are entering into the deepest depth and the highest height of spiritual warfare that any church age has every known. We are matched for the séance people, the spiritualist, the witchcraft people, the ouija board people, the druggers, the punk rockers, and the sex perverts around this world. Honey, you just can't name it and claim it and quote a little scripture. We have got to know this Book. We have to know the author. We have got to have the power of the author. We have got to live in the spirit, or we are going to be on the side somewhere—shipwrecked. I mean it. We are just gonna have to do some more climbing. We really are.

And so I told you last week that fear comes from trespass, because it produces guilt—from the garden 'til now. The thing that produces fear is thought. "The battle is in my brain."

Negative Response—Bondage—Captivity—Torment

I find, myself, when I don't handle things well and I finally climb out of the mud hole, I look back over my shoulder and then I realize that it was just in my head. I allowed that thing to torment the dickens out of me…It was in my head. And if you don't handle it right in your head, it creates an emotional response, which is negative, which leads to bondage, which leads to captivity, which ends in torment. Until you live in terror. You don't want to go to church any more! You don't want to worship! And you wish to God that everybody and everything would just leave you alone.

I know what I am talking about. I get those days. I just wish to God that everybody would just leave me alone. The Lord in His mercy said, "No, no, no, no." And inside I am saying, "I wish you would just leave me alone." People call up and say, "I've just been praying for you." And I feel like saying, "Just shut up and leave me alone. I will handle this." And all the while the Holy Ghost is telling them, "He is not handling this too well, you'd better call him.

Your Level of Knowledge Produces Your Response

So thoughts produce fear, and ignorance also produces fear. Think about the savage in the wilderness laying somewhere, or Africa, or wherever, anything that is not real civilized…if you show the natives of that particular community a camera and the camera flashes, all of a sudden the natives say, "You have stolen my spirit!"

Now you that are knowledgeable say, "What's the matter with you? It is just a negative; it will be done in 60 seconds. Polaroid puts them out right here." And we think their response is absolute stupidity. You must understand; the level of their knowledge is producing their response.

Now, let me say it again for all of those who didn't hear that just then. There is the key to this Bible study: The level of their knowledge is what is producing their response.

While one of the disciples said, "…and Jesus sleepeth…," somebody knows more than the other ones.

Why is everybody boo-hooing and snottin' and cryin' and carryin' on at Lazarus's tomb and Jesus is taking a 4 day leisure trip over there? "If you had only been here…." He said, "I am here now."

See, when you are the Resurrection, what do you care about who dies? Get that? What do you care? If you are the Resurrection, what does it matter if you don't get there for six weeks? The minute that you say, "Get up!" They are getting up! If you have that much knowledge and power flowing in you and emanating from you, what are you worried about some crazy devil-possessed jerk banging his head into the wall? "You are not going to go? "All right, here we go, I am going to wrestle with this dude." No, you're not. You're gonna say, "Hey cut that out." And he will just <poof> stop?

Partial Knowledge is Dangerous

It is when we are not sure; and I am going to tell you something folks, as kind as I can be—partial knowledge is more dangerous than a lot of knowledge. You can know just enough to hurt yourself.

Knowledge is power. Children become afraid of things that adults smile at. And, yet, they are both in the same thunderstorm. The lightening flashes and lights up the sky. You stand there and say, "Boy wasn't that something?" But your kid says, "Good God!" ...looking to hide behind your legs.

I can remember, as a boy, riding the cyclone roller coaster. In those days it was the largest, biggest roller coaster in the world. It was at Coney Island. It was a straight drop, man. No body sat down, you all kind of went up, against it. And your stomach comes up and says, "Hello, how are you?" ...and goes back down. That's the truth! You do not breathe in—going down. You waited until you went up to get fresh air, because everything down there was from breakfast and supper.

I can remember sitting in that, and my dad would take us either in the back seat, or the front seat. You either got the whip, or you got devastated going down. He would sit there and put his arm around me and we would laugh, as that thing would go chug-chug-chug-chug-chug-chug. He'd say, "Look Jeffrey, look at all of Coney Island out there." And I am saying, "Yeah, look at all that, Ferris wheels...steeple chase..." and my other eye was watching as we get to the hill. "Yeah, yeah!" As soon as we got there, I kind of looked at my dad and he looked at me and I went, "hiiiighhhhhhhh." And I just put my face in his chest and said, "All right, let's ride this thing down!" He would laugh all the way down. I was terrified all the way down—holding on. Somehow he knew something I didn't know. He knew there were tracks over the hill. I thought it was the abyss!

Now, I am trying to be humorous so I can reach you. Illustration: When you know something that your child doesn't know, it doesn't cost you as much consternation as them. How many times do we all, as parents, say, "It will be ok." "It's alright." "Don't be afraid." They see a bug, or they see a snake, or they see a lizard. I remember when we started out and Dena saw the chameleon, and OOOHHHH! Here is this thing looking at her, you know, all glued to the window. She was just a little kid. Now a real, real little kid, who doesn't really have any brains, they go eat them and pick them up. They're not afraid of 'em. But when they get a little knowledge, the little knowledge becomes dangerous.

And then you...you come along with further knowledge and say, "Awe, honey, that is just a chameleon," or "that is just a turtle, that won't hurt you." "That won't bother you." They are just filled will horror and trembling and fear, because of their limited knowledge.

Again: The Bible Has a Year's Worth of "Fear Not"

Okay, now let's just turn it around. Now we are children and He is our father. We come into episodes and things in our lives. We, because of our limited understanding and limited knowledge, become terrified. Our father says, "Fear not," 366 times he says, "Fear not." See? We have a hard time with it just like our kids. Okay?

Faith is the antidote for fear. Faith comes from the Word of God. James said, "Receive with meekness the engrafted word, which is able to save your soul." Now let me make myself very clear. It is not sin to be afraid. The devil has told some of you folks, lied to you, that you are just not a spiritual man, boy or girl, because you are afraid. That is a lie! It is not sin to be afraid. It is stupidity to let fear dominate you if you are a child of God. You have 366 promises that tell you, "don't be afraid."

God Puts us in the Middle to Show us it Won't Hurt

Now be honest with me right now, okay? I am out of the humorous thing. I have your attention. Let's just talk serious stuff.... Have you ever got angry with your children when you tried to tell them not to be afraid and they kept...and they kept crying? "...Oh, for crying out loud, stop it...? And you get irritated to the point of—oh come on...you don't get irritated when you have gone about 30 times and tried to tell your offspring the same thing and they just refuse to believe that you are telling the truth? And all of a sudden, your voice changes from tenderness to anger; "I just told you! Come here, it won't hurt you, hold this!"

But I am going to tell you what; God in his mercy sometimes will just do that to us. He keeps saying, "It won't hurt you, don't be afraid, it will be alright." And finally, "Well, I'll just put you right in the middle -- hold onto it."

There are some people that have to handle something before they finally realize their father is not lying. That is what He did in Luke when He appeared and came through the walls; He said, "Don't be afraid. Peace be unto you." They are shaking, man! So what does he do? He says, "Handle Me." "Grab a hold of Me." "I am not a spirit, I am a body." "Touch me." "Put your hands in the holes of the wounds that I suffered for you." "Here, hold me." Now, all of a sudden, the Bible says, "Then were the disciples glad." I'm so glad the Lord deals with us on different levels.

Fear Resists Rationale

Okay. God is for us. He does not give us the spirit of fear. The Bible says He gives us the spirit of power, love and a sound mind. Now, if I understand what it just said, then people who have fear dominating them and tormenting them do not have sound minds. I didn't say they were nutty as a fruitcake, I said they don't have a sound mind. Their mind is tormented. God doesn't give you that. You would not give your children that. You wouldn't take any pleasure in making your children afraid. I am going to tell you something folks, you can hardly reason with people who are afraid. Fear resists any type of rationale.

Be Transformed—Renew Your Mind

Feelings come from us from different viewpoints of our own thoughts. And however we view it, it will end up producing in us a good feeling or a bad feeling...a happy feeling, or a sad feeling. The mind is the playground. How the facts are viewed determines our emotional reaction and response. That is why the scripture says, "Let this mind be in you which was also in Christ Jesus." Then it says, "Let your mind be renewed." You renew your mind by the Word of God. You are not supposed to be conformed to this world, but be transformed. How? By the renewing of your mind, that you might prove that good and perfect and acceptable will of God.

Time For a Recharge

Do you know what that tells you? It just told you that you could have a tremendous victory today and get your teeth knocked out at 6 am tomorrow morning. So what do you have to do? You have to go back to the Book, back to the author and renew again. If your battery cable in your car is not properly attached and you have corrosion there, your vehicle may start great today, and won't even crank tomorrow. And you know if our vehicles breakdown; we say, "Oh, dumb battery!" We need to get it charged.

But when we breakdown, we don't want to get charged. When we breakdown…when we mishandle things, we look elsewhere for the problem…"What is wrong with this truth?" "What is wrong with this preacher?" "What is wrong with our message?" Nothing! Have you checked the battery terminal lately? You know when a car doesn't turn over, I hate for a mechanic to come out and say, "We have got to replace these pistons." "Could we check to see if there is any juice coming through the regulator, the voltage regulator?" "Oh no, I have been a mechanic for 30 years, I always replace the rings, and pistons, and crank shaft." "Just because the car doesn't turn over? Doesn't it maybe tell you that the battery's…." "Hey kid, who's the mechanic here?" "You're sure? Check the battery!"

We Gravitate to, and Become, What Our Mind Pictures

Now I want to show you something. The mind creates images and pictures as it filters information. Whatever picture you cast up, you will gravitate to that and become. I am going to show you something. The images and pictures that are birthed inside of us then give birth to feelings. Feelings will either be faith, or fear; and produce behavior.

Now watch this. Genesis 15: Abraham's story.
(1) "After these things the word of the Lord came unto Abram in a vision, saying," Now, watch the first thing that God's says to Abe. "Fear not, Abram." How come? "I am thy shield, and thy exceeding great reward."

How come God introduces himself to Abraham in a vision with these two great words? "Fear not." It wasn't because Abraham was apprehensive of the presence of God; he was in a vision. It was because of what was going on in Abraham's head. Abraham had been called out ten years prior and he had been given a promise by God saying, "The land you walk through will be your land and I will make of thee a great nation. And if they can number the dust of the earth, so shall thy seed be."

Now for 10 years, Abraham is having mental pictures. So when God shows up, the pictures on the screen are incorrect. So the first thing that God says to Abe is, "Hey, don't be afraid." God doesn't tell us that for future things. He tells us for the ever-present now; which is produced by yesterday. We only have apprehension of tomorrow. You cannot fear that you have apprehension, but you can have fear for now and what was produced from yesterday.

Mental Pictures Produce Feelings; Feelings—Behavior

He was called out. The seed would be like the dust. Sarah was going to be a mommy. Ten years have gone by. Watch this; nothing in the obvious, physical realm has happened, but plenty has happened in the mental realm. For ten years of unfulfilled spiritual promise can play havoc with the mind of the greatest child of God. We live by the Timex, and God just says, "I have made thee a father of many nations." How many babies do you have Abe? And for 10 years he lives with an unfulfilled promise. Do you know what he is doing for 10 years? Mental pictures...mental pictures...mental pictures. Pictures produce feelings. Feelings produce behavior.

(2) "And Abram said, Lord God, what wilt thou give me, seeing I go childless?" Mental picture. What are you going to do for me God? You told me I was going to be a daddy, but I am telling you that I am going childless.

"...And the steward of my house is this Eliezer of Damascus?" And he sees Eliezer as becoming the heir of the promise."

(3) "And Abram said, Behold, to me thou hast given no seed: and, lo, one born in my house is mine heir."

Let me explain what I am trying to tell you. His mind has been active. He has been developing for 10 years mental images and pictures. God was so kind to this fellow, he let him hang himself with his own tongue, 'cause he shows up and says, "Don't be afraid, Abe." They haven't even had a discussion. How did God know the guy is afraid? He sees the screen of his mind and he sees what Abraham has been thinking, because the minute he has a chance, he tells God what he has been thinking...

"I am childless; you haven't kept your word. Hey by the way, I have this Eliezer from Damascus; he's the steward in my house. I guess I am going to die without the promise being fulfilled. Hey, what is going on?"

Abraham says to God, "See here!" That means observe. Then he says in the next verse, Verse 3, "Behold." That means; Hey, take notice of this...as if to say; you ain't taking notice of this, but I have been.

I know where I am going. But I hate for you to miss this point, because this is a good point: He has 10 years of mental images and all he sees is; I am dying unfulfilled. "Now who has told you, you are going to die unfulfilled, Abe?" "These mental pictures...I see myself childless. I see Eliezer, the steward of my house becoming the heir. Man, I am confused." Confusion brings fear. So what does God say to him the first thing? "Fear not."

Fear Causes God to Drop the Shield

Boy, that does something for me that it didn't do for you. He said, "I am afraid I am going to die childless, the promise is going to be unfulfilled." Now watch this. God says, "Fear not." There is a reason why. In Verse 1 He says, "I am thy shield." "I am your present protection and your fear is interrupting that." Let's try it again. "I am thy shield; present protection; but if you keep being afraid, that spirit of fear is going to thwart my desire to be your shield, because you can only function with Me through faith."

What is he saying? When you are afraid, you force God to drop the shield. Now you are susceptible to all kinds of spirits. Watch what else he said...this is awesome: He said,

"I am thy exceeding great reward. I am your future." And your present fear is ruining your tomorrow.

Why are people going to the lake of fire? Read Revelation 21:8. The fearful…read the list…the fearful. What did that fear do for them? Ruin their future. They are going to be cut off forever from God. They are going to be in the lake of fire. And God is telling Abraham, "Don't be afraid." "…Don't give in to this feeling, this emotion." "Don't give in to these thoughts that are giving birth in your mind to crazy stuff, because I am your reward." "I am your shield." "You are going to ruin your today." "You are going to mess up your tomorrow."

Our Brain Lies To Us

When you read it, you read Verse 2 and 3: he spilled the beans… "I am afraid." "I am childless." "You promised I would be the father of a multitude of many nations and dust that couldn't be numbered." "And now I have this crazy Eliezer, he's my steward." He has imagined this in his mind. Eliezer's going to be the heir, but God never told him Eliezer's going to be the heir. Who's lying to this boy? It's in his brain.

It's amazing what tremendous monuments of bridges our minds can build where there's no water. Never been a group of civil engineers like us. We can fight wars when everyone is at peace. Tell me if I am not saying it right, when you walk by somebody in the church and look at them and they give you a funny look and you go, "Well, what's the matter with you?" "Are you mad at me about something?"

Or, if you ain't got the courage to say, "What's your problem, dude?" Then you sit in church and for the next 45 minutes you go, "What is the matter with that jerk?" "...Wonder what that look was about?" And then you sit there, and in 45 minutes you've got the Holocaust on your hand. And it could have been that they just had a real bad day and are just kind of too pooped to participate.... And we read into things...things that are not there. And, I mean, you can feel the tremendous dome of the mosque right in your brain, and all kinds of ornamentation and everything, and have it totally shattered the next time you see that person. They say, "Hey, how are you?" ...and thwwaaaaaaatttttt; you have a legion of contractors in your head that are awaiting your response.

Okay, your feeling, which is resulting from the thoughts of your present situation, is causing a hindrance in my protecting you presently, and it will eventually effect your future. Fear is something we see first, we hear first, and then we feel. And when we feel, we respond and react to it. You cannot receive fear without hearing or seeing. And you cannot receive faith without hearing or seeing.

Faith Comes Only Through Hearing The Word of God

God cannot just walk up to you and say, "Here's a hundred pounds of faith." It doesn't work that way. And we sometimes look for some magical gift that God is going to give us, even when we go to prayer.

"God give me more faith." "God give me more faith." "Lord, help me to believe." "Lord, give me more faith." That is crazy! Faith comes from hearing! You want more faith? Get in this Book until it saturates you...until you can quote it...and inhale it...and spit it out...and chew it...and digest it...and ingest it. Faith comes from the Word of God. It doesn't come from a prayer meeting. I don't care what anybody tells you. I am not going to call them liars; they are mistaken. They are just mistaken.

God isn't just going to come and, POW, give you something. That is crazy! He has given us His Book, just like he gave Abraham his Word. That is His Book. He gave Abe His Word, but 10 years later the Word isn't working for Abraham. He is afraid. What is he afraid of? Afraid of being childless, afraid of dying. Who in the world told Abraham he was fixin' to die?
"…What are you talking about Abe, you're gonna…"
"I am gonna die and he's gonna be…."
"Who told you, you're gonna die?"
"My brain."

Are you ready for this? Do you know where fear comes from, along with your brain? When your body feels lousy. When you are attacked with sickness, or hindrance in your physical being. You could have an imbalance in your pancreas, or you could have an imbalance of insulin or sugar in your body and it will kick off all kinds of chemicals and make you think crazy. There are hormones in female bodies and male bodies that can move and get out of balance, and, man, you are not yourself…giving birth to all kinds of moods. Come on ladies. I married one, I know. I am telling the truth.

The Answer: Replace Fear Image With Faith Picture

Ok, now I have told you the problem. Now I am going to give you an answer. Are you ready for the answer? How do we overcome a fear image? How do we overcome a fear picture? Easy. A faith picture! "A faith picture?" "Oh, I thought you were going to give us a revelation." "I mean; I was really waiting for the seven seals of how old Daniel was when he had the image…" "Oh my God, and who's the guy on the horse...what is his name again?" "Word of God...?" "Well, well, yeah." "Why don't you make it hard, that way we feel like we got something."

That's the problem! Paul's burden, when he wrote to the church, was somehow..."I am afraid lest you just like Eve through the subtlety of the devil would be perverted and fooled and miss the simplicity that is in Christ."

It is so simple, it is profound! The Lord is always talking about the highest plane of faith. It's childlike faith. You just tell a kid..."Yeah, I believe it." You tell an adult..."Oh, let me get my microscope." "Let me send this to the lab." But a kid just says, "Sure!" And goes on and enjoys it. We have to replace evil habits in our lives with good habits, right? We are also charged to replace bad thought patterns with good thought patterns.

Now watch, listen to me, please. I am as serious as Hell is hot, and eternity is long and Jesus is Lord. You have to replace bad pictures in your head with more Word of God that is good. And God gave us the equation and example right here. Now we are talking about the "Father of Faithful." Now, we ought to learn something from the Father of Faith. I'm gonna give you the answer right here:

God Replaces the Eliezer Picture in Abraham's Mind

(4) "And, behold, the word of the Lord came unto him, saying, This shall not be thine heir:" That replaces that image. Ten years he has had it on his head. Eliezer's going to be the heir. Now the Word comes and says, "He ain't gonna be the heir, but he that shall come forth out of thine own bowels shall be thine heir."

Now watch what just happened. I want you to get the equation. The false was cast out. That is not total deliverance. The false image is cast out, the correct image is put in. Never mind saying, "You ought not be this way." We need to say, "Well, how ought you to be."

It is not enough to get out of the world. Honey, you need to get God in you. Watch what he told him. He said, "First I'm going to get rid of that bad image. You've got Eliezer who's the steward, going to be the heir of my promise to you. It's not so." Boom! Take out that image. Now he's got a void. So what does God do? He finishes it. "...He that comes out of your own bowels, he'll be the heir."

(5) "And be brought him forth abroad," now watch this; this is so awesome. and said, "Look now toward heaven, I am going to give you a little help. I am gonna give you an object lesson. I am going to help the mental picture with the aid of a physical picture." Now he takes them out and brings them underneath the canopy of stars. Now watch this, "...and tell the stars, if thou be able to number them..." And you need to understand that is where God's statement stopped. It stopped there. We ran through it, but it stopped there. We need to get the picture. God tells him the new thing. God says, "Eliezer's not going to be.... You're going to have a son of your own bowels...you are going to produce that boy. Boom! Fresh faith is banging in his brain.

"Come here, I want to give you an object lesson, boy." "Get your carcass out here and look at the stars." Now watch what he says...I want you to get how this is written: "Look now toward heaven." Now in order to get faith moving you've gotta take your eyeballs off the problem. Secondly, he says, and tell the stars, or notice the stars. "Look at them." Watch. "If thou art able to number them." See,

God didn't do the rest of that verse right then. It's recorded that way, but that's not the way God did it. He said, "Come out here boy. I put all of this up here. Now look at the stars. You see them? You notice them? Tell the number of them. Start calculating." And God just kinda went, *clunk*, "I'll wait a while."

Abraham is counting; ...873...962...there's 107,942...I mean God is just kinda standing over there going, hmmhmmhmm (laughing under his breath). Do you know why? Because Abraham sees every star as a son...I'm gonna name that one Isaac...gonna name that one Israel...that one's gonna be...that one's gonna be...that one's gonna be...because God has given him a mental picture. And he has a little physical help now. And he sees every one of those stars as his seed. And buddy, this guy's faith is pounding now. It has gone from his head to his heart. It's pounding! And God is going, "Hey, Michael, look at this. Look at Abe. Look at his countenance!"

You have to grasp it, because we don't sometimes take time to count. We're too busy quoting. Read the way it is written...read the way it is written; "Look now toward heaven and tell the stars if thou be able to number them..." So now, while Abraham goes into this new dimension of faith, and he is finally ready to explode, now God starts talking after the pause...and says ..."and he said unto him, So shall thy seed be."

Fill Your Mind With Faith Images

And he believed God was counting on him for righteousness. It replaced fear with faith; bad image with correct image; bad picture with a proper picture. It takes time. You need to read a promise. Stop...Quote...Chew... Meditate... Pause...Think ...Think! Sometimes we just quote scripture; blah...blah.... Mark 11:3-24 ...Matthew 17:11 ...blah...blah...blah...blah. No! Quote it, now chew it, think; create an image. Fill your head. The minute your head is full of faith, the Holy Ghost says, "Oh, here's another shovel full." He's always looking for places where He can deposit more faith.

Either the Problem or Promise Will Produce Picture

Now, watch. We have to either let the promise, or the problem, produce the picture. We have to soak it in. And all of us...let's stop playing spiritual for a second...all of us soak in the problem. You soak enough problems. "...Man, I just been through about 5 days of real bad problems, I've soaked it in 'til it made me sour." So we let the promise produce the picture...soak it in...then the picture will produce the wonder inside you.

If the picture that you produced is a bad picture, if it is a fear picture, it doesn't produce wonder. It produces worry. And you start to worry. "I am so worried...I am so worried...I eat my fingernails to the elbow...I am so worried...."
"Why do you worry?"
"Because of the pictures."

No One Escapes the Onslaught of Fear

Now I have just come out and I am so...I would like to say this before I close. Thank you church for praying for me. I know a whole bunch of you prayed for me. And I know I got my brains beat out last Saturday and Sunday and Monday and Tuesday, and I am out of it. But I know you have all went to the throne and prayed for me. So I am talking to you from a fellow who just knows about worry. You say, "How can the pastor have two bad days?"

"Oh, come pastor with me a little while." "See how many divorces you can handle in a week." "See how many abortions you can handle in a week." "See how many marital problems you can handle in a week." "See how many financial set-backs you can handle." "See how many times you counsel with people who actually go ahead and do everything you told them not to do."

Then, finally, when you are doing everything you know how to do, God says, "I am going to send you in another direction. You've never been this way before." Ha ha ha ha. You go out there and you're kinda looking for; where are the rocks? You go out there and you kinda have a stone face. And so the images in your mind are; "you're crazy being here." "What are you doing?" There is a voice that says, "You're not appreciated."

The Antidote for Worry—Work

And you say, "You're right. Yes, you are right. That's right, I need to go someplace else. That way I won't have any worry." But, I have an antidote for worry. Now don't...wait a minute...wait a minute...just so I can help you. It is not only faith. Faith is the antidote for fear. There's something better for worry. It's Work.

Now, I appreciate you three or four people that showed up Tuesday night when I was finishing the wood chips, let me explain to you why we had the woodchips out there. Twenty-five yards of woodchips. Do you know why? 'Cause I was full of worry. But I said, "Worry! You ain't gonna whittle me down, Worry. I am going to work you into the ground, dude." So I said, "Give me 25 yards of woodchips, I have nothing to do with 12 hours of my day Tuesday, and I'll just spread those woodchips."

So when I spread those woodchips, of course we needed them, so I said, "Devil, I am gonna do something for the work of God that is gonna bail me out of this worry. And I am gonna stand out there and I am going to rake and pitchfork all this stuff in wheel barrels. Fifty different wheel barrels full of stuff, so I can be alone. And I am gonna pray all the time, and I am gonna talk in tongues, and I am gonna cry. I am going to get this mental picture in my brain straight."

And here I am, Wednesday night, fine! But if you worry and don't work, you become frustrated. I'm tellin' you right. I can either suck my thumb with the situation and say, "Well I hope it will go away." It don't go away! You have just got to work your way out of it. You have got to swing and punch and take punches, you've just got to do it! Don't let the dumb thing manipulate you! You manipulate it! You are the one that has the Holy Ghost! You are the Child of God! You are the heir of salvation! You've got the promise! Pour yourself into it and make it obey!!!

Forget the Past—Create A Faith Image

Can you imagine that this fellow starts seeing the stars as children? Can you imagine what God required of this man? Abraham is struggling to believe for one kid. Now he is told to believe for millions. Honey, when you deal with God, He's gonna blow your mind. "…Oh, I just can't handle one kid…." "Here, how would you like a sky full?"

Wow, God! The key is that Satan attacks with fear. We start seeing ourselves losing the battle. We start imaging ourselves as failing. We must find a faith picture. The faith picture is the Word of God. It has tens of thousands of faith pictures. That is why when you read Romans 4:17-21, it says, "Abraham considered NOT the deadness of his own body nor the deadness of Sarah's womb...but was strong in faith, giving glory to God," saying, "...he that has promised is able to perform it." But he had to change the image, the picture. But he got it from God who brings his Word. God did not just go, "Awe, I don't have no problem with fear." No, He gave him Word. Abraham took Word, made a picture. Then God gave him a second picture.

See Yourself As…. Rather Than Feeling

When I knelt down to pray again tonight for this message, I wasn't on my knees 60 seconds—I am taking an estimate—when the Holy Ghost just brought to my mind, as clear as I am looking at you, the woman with the issue of blood. Wasn't even a part of this Bible study, but apparently the Holy Ghost wants me to tell you. There was a woman who had spent all that she had and had grown worse instead of better. But, she heard Jesus was in the vicinity. And the Bible said she said within herself, "If I can touch the hem of his garment, I am going to be whole."

You know what she started out with? She had a picture in her mind! She had created a faith image in her mind! Never mind the past. Never mind the empty bank account. Never mind all the failures and all the diagnosis of the fine medical people of that day. She heard about Jesus and she said, "If I can touch him I am going to be whole." She started out with a picture in her mind!

All God is asking this church is to get a spiritual picture of faith, of what you desire, and what you need, and God will do the rest. You that are sick right now, why can't you see yourself well? You that are under the gun, why can't you muster up enough faith and confidence in Him who has never lied to you, or failed you one time; why can't you right now begin to create a new picture in your mind? And see yourself healed, rather than getting prayed for and feeling something.

Honey, the only reason the lady "felt" was because she already "saw"! Read the instance. The Bible says; the last thing she experienced was she felt in her body she was healed. That was the last thing she experienced! The first thing she experienced, the first thing she had was a faith image—"if I touch the hem of his garment, I am going to be well." My God, she walks down the street with this picture. She's got this picture; "Man, if I ever touch his garment, I am well." "Oh, there I am. Oh, size 10, all right, I am ready. If I can just touch the hem...."

See the End Result in Your Mind

Honey, we need to get a hold of that right now. That is the key to getting healed and delivered and set free from any kind of obstacle in your life. It is to see yourself...the end result. What do you think God is doing with us? My God, we are a tragic looking bunch of folks right now, we really are, but he has looked at us with the eye of faith and said, "Oh, you ought to see the bride when I get her raptured." "You ought to see..." whew, "...you ought to see what she looks like when she is robed on that great getting-up morning...you ought to see what my church is going to be like when I catch her home."

And it is the very image that God has of us that inspires Him to forgive our iniquities and to overlook our trespasses and our shortcomings, because He has an image of us, of what we are going to be like at the end!

Faith Images For Any Time of the Day or Night

Okay, I will run through this real quick. Satan attacks us, brings fear. We need to find a faith picture. Watch this, God told Abraham, "Look at the stars." That means that God gave him an image...a picture at night, and said, "If you have any problems during the day, I will let you look at the sand."

You cannot see stars in the day; you have to see them at night. And when it gets real dark, you can't really see the sand. So He says, "I will give you a faith picture for whatever time you are in." Twelve hours of the day, twelve hours of the night. The Word of God can create an image in your mind that when you are walking during the night, you can see the stars. When you are walking during the day, you can see the sand.

That is why the Bible says, "Jesus is the bright and morning star." Watch: nighttime you can see the star. Watch this, "He is the root and offspring of David." Daytime, you see the root, springing up, growing up. You have an image in bold dimensions.

David Was Fearful, But Overcame

Now what happened? Isaac becomes the product of faith and promise. Fear attacked David through Goliath's appearance and words. Oh, yes! Don't you all believe that David wasn't afraid. Fear attacks the greatest of all of God's people. But the Bible said that he replaced that with a picture. How did David replace it with a picture? Here comes Goliath... "Ho, Ho, Ho, and a bottle of rum. I am gonna knock your head off you little Hebrew punk. I'm gonna cut your carcass in 85 pieces, there ain't gonna be enough left to make a sandwich out of you. You punk."

Watch. Physical frame. He sees. He hears, "I am going to kill you!" Fear. How come he runs at Goliath? He's got faith in his heart. He changes the slide. He goes back and sees a little white-haired man with a long beard and a vial of oil, named Samuel, coming and anointing him saying, "Thou shalt be King." Sees! Hears! Picks out the slide.... "Come on, fat boy, let's tussle!"

Opposed While Working up Faith Image

And unless you can get the image changed in your brain, you will have torment. Fear attacked the disciples in the storm and it shouldn't have bothered them. Just like Bro. Bustard said that time; they should have taken a picture of their arrival. He said we are going to the other side. All they thought was that they were going to Davey Jones' locker. Jesus said, "I will never leave you, never forsake you, never put more on you than you are able to bear."

Okay, David ran from Saul. Why did David run from Saul, and didn't run from Goliath? He got a picture in his mind. He said, "I shall one day perish at the hand of Saul and run away from a backslidden king and run towards a 9½ ft. giant." Why? ...Changing slides. That is why I say that for the best of us, sometimes the machine jams. You think I am kidding you? It jams! And you are doing the best you can to get that in there...like this dumb thing sometimes goes "chunk, chunk, chunk." Sometimes you are trying to put that faith slide in there and you are getting your head beat in while you are trying to get that slide in.

God Helps in Trying Times

Your homework assignment is to study Gideon. Read it. Judges 7. "Oh, thou mighty man of valor." He is behind the barn hiding his shredded wheat for breakfast, and the angel says, "Oh, thou mighty man of valor." You can see Gideon going, "Huh? Me? Me?"

He's a bad self-image. Look at his words, "...If God is among us where are all the miracles?" "How come we are having all this junk with these Midianites and where is all the power of God?" He's tellin' on himself. He is defeated. He is inferior. So an angel comes and brings a Word from the Lord, "...Oh, thou mighty man of valor, go in this thy strength. The Lord is with thee." ...Chunk, Chunk.... "Hey, if that ain't enough for you, go here. Go take your servant Phurah. Go down to the Midianites. They have had a dream. They have had an interpretation to a dream."

We think only Pentecostals can have divine dreams. Ha ha ha. The Midianites had one that night. Yes, they did. Said, "I dreamed a dream, and I saw a cupcake knock over the whole tent." That's what a barley loaf is; it's a cupcake..."I saw a barley loaf roll in and just knock over the whole tent -- laid it on the ground." Can you imagine getting beat up by a cupcake? It is like throwing a bowling ball. Said, "A cupcake rolled in."

And the other guy...you think the first dream is crazy? The other guy who interprets it is way out there! He said, "Ha, this is Gideon. Man the Lord is going to whip us with that cupcake." The Bible says, "When he heard that, he worshiped God, and said, Let's go to battle." The slide was in...Chunk! The sound track was on! Here comes 300 pitchers, trumpets and candles—Victory!!

Thank God for the will of God that we not be tormented by fears and images and feelings and emotions and what people say and what spirits say and things whispered to us. O God, give us the boldness and the courageousness to create in our minds, in our spirits, that faith image that comes to us from the Word of God. Therefore, we will have present protection and our future reward will be secure.

Chapter Four

Let me continue in our little study of fear—Free From Fear.

Psalm 27:1, "The Lord is my light and my salvation; whom shall I fear? The Lord is the strength of my life; of whom shall I be afraid? When the wicked, even mine enemies and my foes, came upon me to eat up my flesh, they stumbled and fell. Though an host should encamp against me, my heart shall not fear: though war should rise against me, in this will I be confident."

Psalm 34:4, "I sought the Lord, and he heard me, and delivered me from all my fears. They looked unto him, and were lightened: and their faces were not ashamed. This poor man cried, and the Lord heard him, and saved him out of all his troubles."

Psalm 56:1, "Be merciful unto me, O God: for man would swallow me up; he fighting daily oppresseth me. Mine enemies would daily swallow me up: for they be many that fight against me, O thou most High. What time I am afraid, I will trust in thee."

Isaiah 26:3, "Thou wilt keep him in perfect peace, whose mind is stayed on thee: because he trusteth in thee.

Peace God's Way—In the Midst of Trouble

In John, the gospel of John chapter 14, Jesus said, "Let not your heart be troubled: ye believe in God, believe also in me."

What did he just say? "Don't be afraid." Then he said in Verse 27, "Peace I leave with you, my peace I give unto you:

not as the world giveth, give I unto you. Let not your heart be troubled, neither let it be afraid."

I've wondered for many years about the terminology, or I should say the phraseology, of the way the Lord stated this. When he said, "Not as the world giveth, give I unto you," I used to read that, and read that, and I said, "Boy, that's kind of a tongue twister how he put that. Why would he do that?" It's because when the world gives peace it's in the absence of trouble. The only way the world has peace is when there's an absence of irritation, or struggle, or anxiety, or problem, or murder, or war.

The only way the world can give peace is when there's an absence of problems. But the Lord said, "I give you peace not as the world giveth." What was he saying? I give you peace even in trouble. See, that's the difference between joy and happiness. Happiness is contingent upon things outside you; trinkets, toys and games. Joy is within. It is true.

Peace in Tribulation

And John 16:33, one last scripture; "These things I have spoken unto you, that in me ye might have peace. In the world ye shall have tribulation: but be of good cheer; I have overcome the world."

"...I've told you these things that in me you might have peace." He said, "in the world you shall have tribulation." What did he just say? You're going to be in the world until you leave here. So, he's already promised you that in the scenario in which you live, you're going to have tribulation. But, "I'm going to give you peace in your tribulation." And that's why you're going to be a question mark to everybody

around you. How come everybody else is eating their finger nails to the elbow and you're smiling like you're on drugs?
Now, we know from the scripture that God is the God of peace. That he imparts to us his tranquility and his peace through knowledge and through spiritual indwelling. And when you can't feel the Holy Ghost, you need to know the word of God.

Now, it's a neat thing when they both kind of climb up on you at one time. You got the *word* and you got the *spirit*. Boy, it's grand. But those times are few and far between. They're just kind of like special times. So most of the time when we fight these things, we fight them through the knowledge of the Lord.

Fear Producers—Ignorance, The Unknown, The Unfamiliar, and the Adverse

Ignorance, the unknown, the unfamiliar and the adverse all produce fear. In the gospel of Mark, Chapter 4, you remember the story, that Jesus said; come on, get in the boat, we're going to the other side. A great storm arose. He was asleep on a pillow in the hinder part of the ship. The Bible says they were terrified, scared and they go and wake him up. They say, "carest thou not that we perish?" Now, watch this; this is what I'm trying to talk to you about—faith. No struggle, no strain, just three words; "Peace, be still." And there's a calm.

That's where we need to get when we pray for the sick and the hurting. Is that calm serenity to get Jesus to come on the scene and just say three little words? Because he's up on the mountain—in the mount of transfiguration—those fellows are down in the valley. They're naming it and claiming it, their quoting it, they're confessing, they're possessing, but they can't get that boy healed. But now watch, He walks in and the whole picture changes. He says, "Bring the boy to me. Come out of him." ...Throws him on the ground, ...comes out of him. That's why we need the faith of the Son of God. I think we'd be less loud, less chiropractic. You think I'm kidding you?

You notice when Jesus stood up on the bow of the boat he didn't scream and yell. He didn't start arguing with the circumstance. He said; "Peace, be still." There's been times when I've been prayed for, that the same thing has happened. Through a fellow brother, or sister, or a minister of Jesus Christ, that the faith of the Son of God just came into the auditorium and there was just a peace that entered into my body, my mind, and it just went...whooooo. No strain.

Jesus stands on the bow of the boat and says, "Peace, be still," and everything changes. He turns to his disciples and says, "Why are you so fearful? Why are you afraid?" They would in essence say; ...well, there's a big storm going on out here and you don't seem to care, you're snoring. How come you're not worried with our worries?

And he just kind of smiles and says; ...what worries you, doesn't bother God. And the Bible says he just says three little words, "Peace, be still." And now all of a sudden they're more afraid of Him. The Bible says, "Now they feared exceedingly, saying one to another, What manner of man is this, that even the winds and the sea obey him?" And they were astonished.

Three Results of Satanic Fear

There are three results of fear. Now here's where our lesson comes from: There is the difference between two fears. The three results of the incorrect fear; *torment, abomination, prevention.* Those three things are the result of satanic fear.

The Bible says in 1 John 4:18, "There is no fear in love; but perfect love casteth out fear: because fear hath torment." Therefore, John is saying, "There is no satanic fear in love." I'm going to try that again, I kind of slipped up on your blindside. God is love. If you and I can be full of God, there is no room for *satanic* fear. The problem with all of us is, we're partial God. We're a few quarts low. We leave room for Hell to come in. We got enough of Heaven to kind of cure our conscience, but not enough of heaven to cure this fear. And when you let fear play with you, fear produces frustration and anxiety and criticism.

Two Types of Fear—Satanic & Godly

There are two types of fear in the Bible. You need to understand, you got to recognize this now. There's *satanic* fear and there's *Godly* fear. One is horrible and one is healthy. Here's how you can decide which is which. If you are tormented, troubled, anxious, worried, fretful, fearful; that fear you are experiencing is not of God. Because perfect love casteth out that kind of fear, because fear has torment. Now, stay with me. That type of fear is satanic.

The Result of Rebellion—Fear

Joshua and Caleb are arguing in Numbers 14:9, for Israel to believe God. And they say twice in Verse 9, "Fear them not, for they are bread for us." ...Don't be afraid of them. The very first two or three things they say in that sentence is, "Only rebel not against the Lord." Now, watch this. Here's where you're going to find where fear comes: after rebellion. "Only rebel not against the Lord, don't be afraid of them." He would have never addressed the fear until he saw that there was rebellion rising up in their hearts. Because when they began to criticize and doubt, doubt gives birth to fear.

Doubt—Faith in the Enemy

You know what doubt really is? You know what fear really is? Faith in the *enemy*. That's why Joshua and Caleb said, "Only rebel not against the Lord." God's already told you, you can have the land. Don't act like a bunch of crazy people. God's done bigger things than this. He brought you out of Egypt. Didn't you see all those dead Egyptians floating in the Red Sea? What have you got, amnesia? "Yea, but these giants are so big." They're not as big as Egypt's power.

In Acts 9:31; we see Godly fear. "Then had the churches rest throughout all Judaea and Galilee and Samaria, and were edified; and walking in the fear of the Lord, and in the comfort of the Holy Ghost, were multiplied."

The Fear of the Lord Brings Comfort

Here's where you're going to find out when you have the fear of the Lord; the fear of the Lord brings *comfort*. The fear of circumstances... man, Satan and situations brings *torment*. You don't have to be a theological Bible school genius to figure out what I just said to you. You can discover it in every situation in your life. You can right away put that fear on the scale and you can find out exactly where it is coming from. But when you fear the Lord, you have comfort. When you are producing inside of you torment, it's satanic.

Remember when you first went to the altar? You were afraid. And it wasn't the fear of the Lord working in you.

No, no, no, no, no. It was satanic fear trying to prevent you from coming. Psalm 2:11 says, "Serve the Lord with fear, and rejoice with trembling." Why? Because we begin to realize how big and powerful and majestic and magnificent God is. This in turn produces reverence and awe and humility in us, which will birth comfort, serenity, tranquility, peace, assurance.

Satanic Fear Chokes Out Love

Godly fear produces comfort, satanic fear produces torment. Godly fear motivates, satanic fear dominates. Now, I found something this morning and I've been reading this book a long time, but when I was reading 1 John 4:18; where it says; "There is no fear in love; but perfect love casteth out all fear," I backed up. And if you'd like to do that for homework...if you would read the previous eleven verses.... It starts about 1 John 4:7, I think it is. From Verse 7, or Verse 8, the next eleven verses until you read 4:18. In those eleven verses, John records seventeen times the word *love*. Now, something just kind of jumped out at me, because Verse 18 seems to be out of place. Because in those eleven verses, seventeen times he talks about love, loved us, the love of God, he loved us, he loves us, He now loves us, we love each other, He loves us.... Seventeen times, he's talking about this wonderful thing called the love of God and then all of a sudden he changes his scenario...stops writing and says, "Perfect love casteth out fear." Doesn't seem to make any sense.

He's talking about love and God loving us and we loving each other and loving the truth and then all of the sudden he just turns around and says; there's no fear in love. Fear has not been in any of the verses previous. But all of sudden he just kind of snatches it out of the air and says, "There's no fear in love; but perfect love casteth out all fear.

He that feareth is not made perfect in love." Why did he do that?

Here's the answer. Fear, if it's allowed to work in any of us, will choke love. And prevent that love from reaching its full manifestation. So here's this apostle writing to us, and he's telling us all about the love of God and how he loved us and gave his life for us and we should love each other, love the brethren, love the body and to love the truth because he loved us..."Wherewith a great love he loved us." And all of a sudden the Holy Ghost goes; boom! And he goes; "Fear hath torment. Perfect love casteth all fear." What in the world is he doing?

We're getting a signal from the Holy Ghost! Fear can prevent the love of God from reaching its full demonstration in the best of us. And so the Holy Ghost tries to get a hold of us through the pen of this Apostle John saying; hey, if you're really going to have the love of God in you, you've got to handle this fear thing...because if you let fear work in you, it's going to abort the fullness of the love of God.

Divine Love Cannot be Demonstrated Where Satanic Fear Is In Place

There's another problem with this. Not only does fear choke love from its full manifestation, but if you allow fear...and I allow fear to operate in my life, my mind, my actions...divine love cannot be demonstrated when satanic fear reigns. And if you read that scripture and tie it in to what Jesus said previously, "By this shall all man know that ye are my disciples if you have love one to another." But if you're tormented by fear, the world sees among us; frustrated people. They don't see the witness of love.

I'm just going to hang myself with a bunch of preachers right now. I have a firm feeling that some of our fine brethren who are so adamant that they run their churches with an iron hand and they're against everything but fresh air; I have a sneaking suspicion that they're full of *fear*. And they're insecure and they can't manifest love, so they become tyrants for Jesus, because fear dominates.

If I just make the rules rigid enough and I raise my eyebrows, or crunch 'em down, and I just project that image...boy, you're going to have to deal with me if you keep messin' around, you're just kind of hard now.... Of course, you'll never be happy. But then again, you can either be happy or live by the rules. And at the same time, may I just put a plug in for rules? I think we need them. I think we need guidelines and perimeters. I think we need some type of circumference in which we can see what is no-man's land and what is dangerous. I really do think that we're supposed to live in obedience to the King. All the preacher is, like an Old Testament, or New Testament prophet, ...he just gives direction.

Fear, Being a Spirit, Has Personality

You're business really isn't with Jeffrey Wayne, it's with Jesus Christ! He's the King! I'm just the voice. The thing is, if you don't love the King, the King sends the voice to correct you. Why? So, you can get back into a love relationship with the King. I'm telling you the truth. Fear, according to the Bible, fear is a *spirit*. Oh yes, it's a spirit, because it has personality. Oh yes, it has. There's a personality behind fear. It is not just an emotion. That's why the Bible said, you got to cast out fear. You can't cast out an emotion. That's stupid. "I'm going to cast out jealousy." You can't do that! "I'm going to cast out anger." You can't do that!

Only Spirits Can be Cast Out

Now, you can cast out a *spirit* of anger, a *spirit* of jealousy. The Bible talks about a husband in the Old Testament; "If a spirit of jealousy come upon him." You can deal with a spirit. You can cast a spirit out. But you can't cast an emotion out. Watch what I'm telling you. Fear is a spirit; it has a personality. Why? Because God is love and God is a Spirit and He has a personality. So, how do you cast out a spirit of fear? With the Spirit of God!

The Three 'C's' To Victory:
Cast **Out Spirits—***Crucify* **Flesh—***Confess* **Sin**

Let me give you, again, the three "C's" to victory. If you're dealing with sin, you cannot cast sin out. We pray for people that smoke cigarettes, we pray for people who drink, we pray for people who maybe have sexual fantasies, play games in their minds, we pray for people who do dumb things. And they say, "I got a real problem with cigarettes, I want you to pray for me." And I've prayed for probably thousands of people and now that I'm getting to be older and I realize, …I wasted my time. 'Cause you don't need to pray over somebody's cigarettes, you need to just stop smoking them. 'Cause what you're asking is for a preacher to do your dirty work for you 'cause you ain't got the courage, or the discipline to take care of yourself. Because if you have a problem with your flesh, you're not supposed to do anything with your flesh but crucify it.

"Well, I got a tobacco demon in me." "Well, I can take care of that; I can cast the demon out of you right now." …Guarantee you're still going to smoke, 'cause you want to…. "You mean you wake up in the morning with that in your mouth?" "Oh yeah, the devil puts it in my mouth." "Well, spit it out and adhesive-tape your mouth shut and just praise God!" You think I'm kidding you? We've had frustrated people in the millions among us 'cause we're tryin' to cast out things you're suppose to crucify. When you deal with sin, you don't crucify sin and you don't cast sin out. The Bible says; you confess your sin and the blood of Jesus Christ cleanses you. 1 John 1:9; "We are cleansed by the blood of the lamb, the washing of the word." You cleanse sin, you don't cast it out and you don't crucify it. You cleanse it. When you're dealing with flesh, you crucify it.

Galatians 5:24, "And they that are Christ's have crucified the flesh with the lusts thereof." If you got a wandering eye, don't blame the devil, you need some personal discipline, you idiot! If you happen to have a weakness in your life for A, B, C, or D, for crying out loud; don't pray until you talk in tongues, just stop doing that! It's the devil!

Go on a two or three day fast, you people that inhale seventy-five cups of coffee a day and see if it's the devil, or caffeine. Try it! "Now, Lord you just give me the victory over this caffeine, Lord." I've heard people pray a caffeine demon. Caffeine demon? You mean, every morning you meet a demon in your cup and you mix sugar and sweet-n-low in with him and say, "Hi ol' demon, how you doing? Come on in me." Well, that's ignorant!

"Pray for me, that I just get the victory over this nicotine devil, this caffeine devil, this sugar free devil." Well, that is so stupid! You get addicted to that stuff. Your body does...your chemical composition and make up...and you just turn around say, "Bless God, I'm fasting tomorrow." And those little things inside you...they're not devils! The chemical reactions in your body just go, "...ahhhhh, give me coffee. I will kill you if you don't give me coffee by eleven o'clock." And you have to talk to your flesh.

"...You're not eating today." Oh, yes I am. Give me a bologna and cheese with a pickle and potato chips or I will kill you."

It's Not the Devil—It's Flesh

It's like you're having a conversation with a little person that lives inside you. But, it's not a devil. Listen to me! We have dealt with, "That's the devil doing that." No, it's not!! How can you have a bologna and cheese devil? How can you have a jelly donut demon? What kind of crazy foolishness is that! It's the chemical composition of your body. And your flesh has learned to be indulged and pampered. When you tell that flesh, "No...." That flesh says, "Oh yes!!" You think I'm kidding you? We had four people at prayer this morning. I wonder whose flesh won? I'm talking about you that weren't here.

"...I'm going to get up in the morning at six o'clock, 'cause I need to pray." Boy, that alarm rings and your body just goes, "Calm yourself, child. You have a hard day ahead of you." And you say, "That's right, I really do. That's right, bless God. God knows my heart." You oughta get out of bed. And you say, "You know, the devil just made me sleep late."

You Will do for Gold What You Won't for God

He didn't do no such a thing, you lazy slob! You just didn't roll out of the sack! Now, if there was *money* involved, you would've went. If you got fifteen bucks an hour to pray, I'd have a house full tomorrow. You think I'm kidding you? You'll roll out of the sack for gold, but you won't do it for God!
"Well, I got to go to work."
"Why?"

"That represents money."
"What do you think prayer represents?"
"Well, it sure ain't money."
"No, but it's treasure, it's growth, it's maturity, it's discipline, it's character, it's life. Truth."

I'm not trying to damn and condemn anybody. And I'm not trying to make you feel bad. I'm trying to get you to understand that you absolutely hurt yourself when you blame the wrong thing. It's so easy to just blame this mystical, magical, invisible thing called a demon. When all it is, is a lack of self-discipline and crucifying the flesh.

You get a poor guy that's used to drinking beer every night and booze every weekend and wine, or whatever and all of sudden he just goes on the wagon, "...man, the guy's got DT's. He's got the shakes, man...the trembles." It's not because he's got a devil. It's because his body composition and his mind-set has got used to a certain lifestyle and now he's aborting it.

Spiritual Problems Can Produce Sickness

You're dealing with the flesh, you got to crucify the flesh. You have to crucify the flesh! But, if you are dealing with a spirit, you cannot crucify a spirit, you got to cast it out. I am being more and more persuaded, as we fail more and more in our praying for the sick, that we are misdiagnosing a lot of people's problems; that we'll have more victory when we get ready to pray for people if we take a few minutes to diagnose the problem, because a lot of problems have a root of bitterness in them. They have a spiritual problem in them, they have an area somewhere in their life that hasn't been forgiven. And when those things are operative below the surface, they can produce sicknesses. I'm telling you the truth.

Living in Obedience to God Negates the Devil's Torment

Okay, Mark 16 & 17, Jesus said that we're supposed to cast out evil spirits. We've talked to you for a few moments about torment; the spirit of fear torments you. Now, the Bible says the spirit of fear dominates people; it dominates people. King Saul was Israel's first king. He was oppressed. Why? He was living in rebellion to God. The scripture says the Lord sent an evil spirit to him. What does it mean when it says the Lord sent an evil spirit? God allowed the protection of Abraham's covenant to get off Saul, because he was living in rebellion. And so God allowed an evil spirit to come torment him. Which means; if you live in obedience to God, there is no way a devil can torment you.

Say what you want to, in a lot of areas in our lives, we have major problems and minor problems, because we live in rebellion to various principles of scripture and it produces problems in our lives. Saul was tormented. If he had gone to Shand's hospital they would've said he was a maniac. He was having seizures. But we know from the scripture that although the seizure was a fleshly demonstration, the root problem was a spirit. And when that spirit came on him, it gave him an improper behavior pattern.

Do you know why the Lord let an evil spirit come to Saul? ...The goodness of God. ...To awaken him, to make him see his desperate need and bring him to a place of repentance. But it never brought him to repentance, so he ended up dying lost. He wouldn't repent.

Fear has the ability to hold you back from doing Gods perfect will; from fulfilling his purposes for my life and yours. Look at the fear of God, instead of satanic fear.

Now, remember, that satanic fear that was allowed to touch King Saul, tormented him. He grabbed his head and he'd wait for the music to play. He'd get David, ...play, ...calm his spirit. We'd say he's having a fit, ...nervous breakdown. And then David would come in and play his little violin, or harp, or ukulele or whatever he played, and all of a sudden he'd get calm again. He'd be okay.

Godly Fear Brings Liberty

But now look at the Godly aspect of Godly fear. The Bible said that Noah being warned of God, moved with fear, to the building of an ark and the saving of his own family. Why? Because Godly fear, contrary to popular opinion, does not bring bondage, it brings liberty. Godly fear motivates to action. To move with fear, Godly fear; means a reverence, an awe, towards the holiness of God. It doesn't mean putting your hands up, being scared to death and doing what He says so He doesn't throw you in a lake of fire.

We may start out that way serving the Lord. That we're afraid of being judged and damned to a devil's Hell. But that's only elementary, for the Bible says, "The fear of the Lord is the beginning of wisdom." It's the beginning of wisdom. The fear of the Lord, one writer says, is the beginning of knowledge. But fools despise wisdom and instruction. So the Godly fear that came to Noah was healthy. It was a healthy reverence, he moved with fear.

Two Fears—One Dominates, The Other Liberates

One type of fear dominates and gives you bondage. The other fear liberates and gives you power to accomplish. It's easy to recognize which fear you're experiencing. Watch. There's something else that fear does. Fear...well let me finish this up. Fear dominates. The Bible says, "The fear of man bringeth a snare." King Saul was told to kill all the Amalekites. When he gives his answer to the prophet he said, "I was afraid because of the people." They said, "Let's spare the best stuff," and the majority rule won. King Herod, the Bible said, "Feared John greatly and did many things because of him." That was an awesome fear.

But, when Salome danced, if that was her name, when his daughter danced and he was half bagged and she asked for John's head, he regretted his own, watch this, nevertheless because of them that sat there. "The fear of man bringeth a snare." He was tormented in his mind, "...Boy, I look bad, I won't get in the good poll this week. If they realize I broke my word to my kid, man I'll never be able to go to this people." Because he governed by fear, anyway. So now, fear grabs a hold of him and he kills the best thing in his life. I know what I'm telling you. When you have the fear of God, I told you, it produces comfort.

There's not a doubt in my mind, Shadrach, Meshach and Abednego were afraid of the furnace and afraid of the king's edict, but they feared God more. So then they could answer and say; we're not afraid of what you do to us and what you say O' King, we fear the Lord. And they literally walked into the furnace. They had a comfort and a serenity and an assurance.

Fear of God—Reverence—Brings Comfort

Same thing with Daniel and the lion's den. Same thing in the book of Exodus with the midwives who greatly feared the Lord. Here's what I'm trying to tell ya, the fear of the Lord is healthy. It produces a comfort, it produces an assurance. It is good to fear the Lord. Now, I don't mean looking at God like he's a cop, I mean the wonder and amazement and grandeur of what God is. To think that He's for you; that everything He's ever done has been for your benefit; that He'd never leave you, nor forsake you, nor put anything on you that's too great for you to bear. He'd make a way to escape; it's all for you! That oughta produce a fear, a reverence, an awe, in your heart, which produces comfort.

You catch yourself eating your fingernails to your elbow, you need to stop in your tracks and say, "That's the devil." Worry and anxious and oh, oh, oh, "...that's the devil." Fear hath torment. Noah didn't have any torment, Daniel and the three Hebrew children didn't have any torment; King Saul had torment. Herod the King, he had torment. John didn't have any torment.

Peter's asleep in jail, he's afraid he's going to get his head cut off? No, he fears the Lord. Wasn't it David who said, "Though I walk through the valley of the shadow of death, I will fear no evil." What? Now, wait a minute. He gives you the answer why he will fear no evil, "For thou art my...... Your presence, your rod, your staff, they comfort me."

Only the Fear of the Lord Brings Comfort

The fear of the Lord brings comfort. It brings confidence, security, assurance. I'm going to tell you something folks, there's too many of us Pentecostals living a life worrying about being lost. I'm going to violate your theology...But you ain't supposed to live your life worrying about being lost! You're not supposed to, everyday say, "Oh God, I wonder if I've sinned today, or had a bad thought, or did something wrong, or the sin of omission. Oh God!" You're tormented!

We need to be established in the righteousness of God. If we're born again of water and spirit and we're in Christ and Christ is in us, nothing can separate us from the love of God. Nothing! You say, "Well, I know people that backslide." Nothing separated them from the love of God, they walked away! But no devil took them away. No man took them away. No organization took them away.

The Importance of a Daily Prayer Life

Hear what Jesus said, "I give unto my children eternal life and no man can pluck them out of my hand. My Father which gave them me is greater than I am and no man can pluck them out of his hand." Sounds like eternal security! It's supposed to be eternal security! We are not supposed to eat our fingernails to the elbow, worrying if we are backslid by the time we go to bed. Folks, if we live in the Holy Ghost, that is why it is so important that we have a daily prayer life and we walk with God and we are honest, and pure, and sincere, and we are Word people, and we are prayer people, and we are tongue-talking people.

Come on, now. God's put on Calvary to get a house full of New Jerusalem. Now are you going to tell me that if we start to fear in the wrong way, God is going to say to us; ...Well, you ought not to have done it that way....Go to Hell, you dumb fool....

He won't do that. He will do this; ...Hey come here. Hey, come over here. Hey preacher, go over there. Hey, scripture, get a hold of them. Hey gospel song, get a hold of them. Hey, witness, Hey something, Hey conscience.... Honey, you are loved by a love that will not let you go. You are going to have to fight your way to get to a devil's Hell, my friend. Calvary was for you. And if you can learn how to rest and relax in Jesus Christ you wouldn't be so hyper and negative in your faith and so frustrated.

Don't Struggle—It's Easy to Live for God

Too much stinking, struggling going on among us. It ought to be easy to live for God. The Bible said the way of the transgressor is hard. It is not hard to live for God. Relax in the Holy Ghost.

Well, I might as well just hang myself completely. We preachers have made it hard on you poor slaves. You live by this, boy, or you got me to answer to. Now I believe in standards. Now don't you liberal-minded dudes walk out of here and go lay naked on 39th Avenue. I hope somebody runs you over. I believe in standards. I am going to believe in them until Jesus says it's ok for my wife to go around in mini skirts and short hair and for herself hanging out and everything else. But until the Lord tells me that, she is just staying dressed the way she is. I don't care what all you liberal cats do. You can play your dirty little nudey games and do it all you want to. I am not going to do it. But that is not my salvation. And that is not my security. I do that because I fear the Lord and I want to please God and I am trying to find a lifestyle that is not only pleasing to God, but it is comfortable to me.

Live Comfortably in the Holy Ghost

We have got to find a place that we don't violate scripture, or violate the Holy Ghost and, yet, can be comfortable. We somehow think that living for God is wearing sackcloth. Let's be comfortable, I have to believe Adam was comfortable. Comfortable—not sloppy. You see, people misconstrue. Well, sloppy. No, Oh no, no, no, no. I'm comfortable in a certain lifestyle. I don't like to wake up in the morning and say, "Oh God, I wonder if I am lost?" God doesn't enjoy that and I don't enjoy that. You have a bad thought that comes in your mind, or you react a certain way, or you miss an opportunity, or you mishandle something...if you are not careful you let the stinking devil put guilt on you that will produce fear in you. Then you have anxiety and then you have torment.

Now, see, the other danger of that spectrum is that people say, "Jesus paid it all and live any sloppy hellatious, horrible life you want to." You can't do that either! But there is a place... there is a place in God that if I am honest and sincere...if I am honest in my praying and my studying and I am pure in my confession, that I can still make mistakes and be comfortable. You people whose children never communicate with you...you know why they don't? They are uncomfortable with you. And that doesn't mean that you have to be a sugar daddy and a sloppy idiot and always giving into them.

God's Purpose—Save You and Others Through You

Last thing I want to tell you: fear prevents, it torments, it dominates, it prevents. God has a two-fold objective: He wants to save us and then He wants to save others through us. Now watch this, because if you haven't liked anything yet, you will like this. It will be deep theological, but you will like this one.... Two objectives: God wants to save you and wants to use you as a vessel of honor to save others. How does He do it? Through the Holy Spirit, which brings comfort, which you receive by faith.

Now wait a minute. The Bible says the love of God shed abroad in our hearts by the Holy Ghost. That is how you get rid of the fear; the love of God shed abroad in your hearts by the Holy Ghost. Satan also has two objectives:

prevent you from being saved and prevent you from being used for the salvation of others. How does he do it? He uses spirit also—fear. Boy, I thought you theological dudes would jump high! Fear of people's opinion, fear of peer pressure, fear of rejection....

You Cannot Inherit What Faith Gives Until You Overcome What Fear Produces

Why don't people serve the Lord? Why do some of your wives and husbands and children, why don't they serve the Lord? What is their problem? Oh, they have fear of peer pressure, fear of a changed lifestyle and fear of this and fear of that. That is all it is. We are called to enjoy the Kingdom of God, but we receive the Kingdom of God by inheritance. Listen to me carefully. You cannot inherit until you overcome. "He that overcometh shall inherit all things." You cannot inherit what faith gives until you overcome what fear produces.

What You Don't Overcome Dominates You

What you don't overcome, overcomes and dominates you. Romans 6:16-18, that is what it says. "Know ye not, that to whom ye yield yourselves servants to obey, (Yield yourselves) his servants ye are to whom ye obey: (To whom you obey) whether of sin unto death, (Right) or of obedience unto righteousness?" 17: "But God be thanked, that ye were the servants of sin, (Right) but ye have obeyed from the heart that form of doctrine which was delivered you." 18: "Being then made free from sin, ye became the servants of righteousness."

See? Whatever you don't overcome dominates you and prevents you from becoming what God wants you to be. Okay. Fear keeps Christians from possessing what Jesus purchased for them. That is why the majority of Christian churches do not practice and preach divine healing. You know why? They are afraid they will fail. I am going to tell you something. The Lord Jesus gave me a commission to preach the gospel to the whole world and the gospel saves, but if I take that scenario of opinion, then I am not going to preach anymore. Most of the people I preach to, don't get saved. And yet, the message I offer saves.

Obey the Word—Leave the Results to God

Jesus, with the parable of the sower, said only one out of four is ever going to get saved. Think with me. The Bible said Jesus appeared unto 500 brethren at one time, yet, when the Holy Ghost fell, only 120 were there. That is about 1 out of 4. Jesus Christ, that was brutalized and beaten and stripped and bruised for us, so that we could be healed...majority Christianity is afraid, so they don't even practice it. Those of us that are trying to practice it and we get befuddled and frustrated when people die, when people stay sick, when people are still hurting...sometimes you get afraid and say, "what is the sense in trusting God?" "It doesn't seem to work." But that is what we were told to do. So I will pray for another thousand and maybe five will get healed, I don't know. I just keep extending myself, though I get into a deeper dimension and a power level of understanding what God is trying to do.

Jesus Said, "Fear Not"

My God, if we believe that in healing, why don't we believe that with people with the Holy Ghost? We have a generation that Jesus bled and died and resurrected, ascended, sent back the Holy Ghost for and the majority of Christianity does not receive, nor believe in the gift of the Holy Ghost. Why? Afraid! "We don't want no wildfire here." "We don't believe in tongues." And they refuse the very thing that is theirs. Where did they get that fear? It is not a good reverence fear for God. It is satanic. Jesus said in Luke 12:27-32, "It is the Father's good pleasure to give you the kingdom. Fear not." That is what he says. It begins with 32; "Fear not, little flock; for it is your Father's good pleasure to give you the kingdom." And all that pertains to the kingdom. "What time I am afraid, I will trust in thee." (Psalms 56:3)

The fear of man is a snare. Fear has torment. The fear of God brings comfort. Help us Lord to recognize when it is your fear and when it is Satan's fear. I pray for these people, for everybody that is here. If there is anybody here that is suffering from a spirit of fear, by my confidence and my faith in the Word of God, I bind that spirit of fear. I command it to leave that body in Jesus' name. I command it to cease and desist from tormenting any of your children. O God, help us to recognize what is a spirit and what is flesh and the difference between flesh and what is sin. O God, you don't want us, Lord, to live frustrated, anxious, worry-filled lives. O, teach us to rest in the Holy Ghost. (Tongues & Interpretation at end of service)

"I have taken them and delivered them and turned them loose from the things that bothered them most. I have touched eyes that were blind. I have touched hearts that were broken and I have reached deeper and I have touched the innermost. I have touched the fears of the heart of the people that were disturbed, that were tormented. I, the Lord God, have visited my people regularly and given unto you a deliverance. It is not My will that you be tormented. It is not My will that you be anxious. It *is* My will that you could enjoy this that I have given unto you, that you could be happy, that you could rejoice in your being, that you could be empty of the tormenting fear that has come upon you. Rejoice in Me. I say, Rejoice in Me. Rejoice in Me, for I have set you free. Rejoice...."

Chapter Five

Fear Will Come, But Don't Be Dominated By It

It is not a sin to be afraid. It is not a sin to be afraid, but...you shouldn't be dominated by fear.

2 Timothy 1:6, I found something very unusual today in studying that I never had really caught on to before and I'm just going to put it out there and let you make your own decision. Paul is writing to his son Timothy in the New Testament and he said something very unique. He says, "Wherefore I put thee in remembrance that thou stir up the gift of God, which is put in thee" ...not the revival, not the evangelist, not the pastor, not the preacher, not the special camp meeting; he said, "I tell you, you stir up the gift that's in you." You do it! ...Says, "stir up the gift that is in you by the putting on of my hands."

Apparently, and I'm saying *apparently*, from this scripture Apostle Paul imparted to Timothy, either a spiritual gift, or some type of faith impartation. Where he said, "...you received it by the putting on of my hands," or he could be referring to the fact that he prayed Timothy through to the Holy Ghost.

In Apostolic days, the impartation of the Holy Ghost was done by the laying on of hands. It ought to be done that way right now! Something was done to Timothy via Paul by laying hands on him and praying for him, and he says, "Okay, now stir up the gift of God." Now, my opinion is that I think it's making reference to the fact that it's the Holy Ghost. For the Holy Ghost is the gift of God. It is! It's the gift of God, so he goes a little further and says something very strange now. He says, "Now stir up the gift of God that's in you that was given to you by my putting my hands on you when I prayed for you." Then he says, "For God has not given us a spirit of fear."

Why does he put that in there after he just told them to stir up the gift of God that's in you, unless somehow Timothy was afraid? That's why he first started with, "stir up the gift that's in you." And then he goes on to say, "For God has not given us the spirit of fear but of power and love and a sound mind." Now, why would he say to his son of the Gospel, "God has not given us a spirit of fear but of love and power and a sound mind"? Why is he saying that to him? Not to just be filling pages in a book. There must be a present problem.

Stir Up The Gift *to Combat Fear*

So he's addressing his son of the Gospel in love. Not in condemnation; in love, telling him, "Hey, when you got this gift of God when I prayed for you, now somehow it's dormant, because you're acting afraid of something. But God hasn't given us the spirit of fear, but of power and love and a sound mind." He's telling Timothy that. Now watch this. "Be not thou therefore ashamed of the testimony of our Lord"…now that can make you afraid, peer pressure; go to pray in public and it's a Jewish holiday; it's the Passover.

I've been with some of you…want to witness for the Lord and all of a sudden what happens to some of you? A spirit of fear. You know what the spirit of fear will tell you when you want to witness for the Lord? "Later. This just ain't the right time." Well, what exactly would be the right time? I'll let you know. Watch this. "Be not thou therefore ashamed of the testimony of our Lord, nor of me His prisoner."

Fear comes by associating with whackos. Now I'm saying this with all due respect to Apostle Paul. To this world and the world he lived in, he was an absolute left-field whacko. Now by that I'm saying he was extreme. And so when you're associated with him, honey, you got some stares. So he says, "Don't be ashamed of me the Lord's prisoner." Why would he say that to Timothy unless there was a situation?

See, we're living in a generation that wants to slip up on the blind side of people—catching them in the Gospel net and actually making them think they're going fishing. And I don't know if Jesus' concept would say, "Okay, let's handle this right now." ...and Boom! ...and thousands of people just walked away from Him and just left Him in the dust. Why? Because he was just so straightforward. "...this is what it takes to be saved." Boom! "Follow me and they're going to hate your guts." "They'll probably nail your hide up to a cross. You'll suffer for the Gospel. Few friends...be a tough time." Boom! And the crowds disappeared.

God Can Do What We Can't

Now we got this new system. We just kind of hide it. And then about nine months later, when they get used to being with us, then we spring it on them. I don't think that's good. I do think we have to have some kind of wisdom. Now you have to understand what I'm telling you. The Lord could do some things dealing with people that poor old Jeffery Wayne and some of thee cannot do. I'll tell you why.

What was recorded of Him, He knew what was in man and needed not for any man to tell Him. So when he looked at people He was looking at better than an x-ray. He knew their physical, mental, and psychological make-up. He could look right at them and say: This one can take it and that one can't. This one's fake as a nine-dollar bill and this one has a weakness in this area: and He dealt accordingly. Well, that ought to tell us something.

We cannot just blanketly deal with people. But, as you feel after the Spirit, you pick up on people and how to deal with them. "He that winneth souls is wise." There are some people that you can deal with them about their sins and literally punch them in the nose…"Hey Stupid!" Pow! "Cut that out fool!" And they'll just take it. And there are other people that you can say, "Hey, we don't believe in that" and they'll leave.

Now, to put the icing on all that I just said: I still think we need to be honest and up-front with everybody. To what degree we reveal things, we need a prayerful attitude. Come on, we might as well be honest, we tried to scale too many fish and hadn't caught them. We tried to skin too many hides and hadn't got the hide in the trap. Here we go…we tried to make too many people Pentecostals. We need to just try to make them Christians!

Don't Be Ashamed—But Be Partaker—of Afflictions of The Gospel

Okay, watch this… "Nor of me his prisoner: but be thou partakers of the afflictions of the Gospel according to the power of God." Now if I'm reading this right, Paul is concerned that apparently—and I'm saying if I'm reading this right—apparently Timothy had a fear that was apprehensive because of the persecution that was arising for being a Christian. That necessitated Paul to write, "Now don't be ashamed and don't be overwhelmed, just be a partaker of the afflictions of the gospel." Why is he saying this to that man? So he won't be bowled over by it, or he won't let in fear because of it.

Overcoming Fear

Let me give you one more lesson: Let me see if I can put the icing on the cake. My last one is overcoming fear permanently. Overcome who? Overcoming fear, permanently. As I taught you in previous lessons, fear is a *spirit*. It shows itself in the *emotion* of fear. But the Bible says that God has not given us a spirit of fear, but a spirit of power, love, and a sound mind. So the spirit of fear doesn't come from God, it comes from the devil. There's satanic fear and there's Savior fear. One is healthy and one is evil. The one that's satanic comes from the devil, satanic fear brings torment and domination and prevents you from doing what you want to do in your whole life. It curtails your activities. It fills you with consternation.

Let The Love of God Overcome Fear

Where the spirit of fear isn't, there is honor and reverence and respect for your God...helps you be liberated and gives you a privilege to participate. It's not bondage. It's liberty. Fear is a spirit. God is a Spirit. God is also called in the scripture, the Word. "The Word was with God and the Word was God." The scripture also says God is love.

1 John 4:18 says, "Perfect love casteth out all fear." So what are we saying? That when the spirit of fear comes upon us we need to let the love of God permeate us. And sometimes you can do that with a whisper, and sometimes you got to do it with a wrestling match. But listen to me folks, if you don't fight, you're taken slave. And some of you right here tonight have a problem with fear, because you won't fight. You have to fight! If you don't fight,

you're a pawn. But you have mighty weapons with which to fight. I'm not talking about naming and claiming.... I'm not talking about *positive human attitude*, and human *will* over devils.... That's a bunch of foolishness! I'm talking about scriptural foundation to fight!

We Need to be Filled With Love of God

Now watch this. Here's what we need to do to get permanent victory over fear: we need to ask God to fill us with His love. Now stay with me. Not loving others, nor asking as I've done...maybe you've never done it, but I've asked God in prayer..."Lord help me to love you more." " Lord I don't feel like I love you like I ought to...." That's not the love I'm talking about. I'm talking about the love of God himself: In other words the essence of His nature, for His nature is love.

We need to ask God to fill us with His love. Sometimes I've prayed for God to let me be full of His love. Why? So I could love others. Wrong motive! "Oh God give me a burden so I can serve and do..." ...wrong motive. If I can get full of the love of God I *will automatically* carry a burden. I will automatically be sacrificial. I will automatically desire the deepest secret of my heart—to be pure. You get what I'm saying? Maybe nobody has talked to you this way. But when I was here this afternoon in prayer, I was just walking about here just asking God to fill me with the love of God. I know the Bible says, "The love of God is shed abroad in our hearts by the Holy Ghost." But I mean to be full of just His love. Let me sense it. Let me feel it. Let it do something to my drives and my emotions, because perfect love...and that's Him, He's perfect love...casts out fear. And fear has all kinds of stepchildren like apprehension and anxiousness and worry. They're all relatives to fear.

Fear Has Many Relatives

Let me tell you something friend, down the line about three generations, another relative of fear is *criticism* and *murmurings* and *complaining*. They're down about three generations, but they're hooked onto the family. And somewhere in there is *disappointment*. And all that stuff is born from fear. Now get what I'm saying. God, fill us with the love of God. I have to take a guess that there are not a handful of us in this whole church that has ever just stayed for a while in prayer and just asked God for nothing but to be full of the love of God. "Lord let me be full of the love of God."

Look, Paul wrote to one church and said, "It is my prayer that you might be filled with all the fullness of God." They had the Holy Ghost! They had the gifts and signs and wonders and miracles! They were baptized in Jesus' name! But to be filled with the fullness of God…! …you know what I'm talking about? I'm trying to help you. I'm trying to help myself. Just think if you get bathed in just that awe, that aura of the love of God…and you're going to worry? You're going to worry and fret? You're going to be anxious? You're going to be filled with consternation? Impossible!

Well now, if you say, "Amen and bless God, that's right," and you're sitting here tonight and eating your fingernails to the elbows, that ought to tell you about the measure of oil in your life. Now, you may *leave* here with a black eye, but I *came* here with two.

Unforgiveness Brings Torments

I want to show you something that I've never seen before. I don't have time to go to Bible school; I'm in Bible school. Matthew 18: 34-35, this was the servant that had been forgiven the great debt. Remember? Then he goes and chokes that poor guy that only owed him a few pennies. But watch this, I never tied this together until today; "And his lord was wroth and delivered him to the tormentors till he should pay all that was due unto him. So likewise shall my heavenly father do also unto you"...we blame the devil, but it was the hand of God... "If ye from your hearts forgive not every one of his brothers their trespasses...." Some of us tonight are having trouble with fear. Fear hath torment. The scripture says this fellow is delivered to the tormentors, plural: Fear, anxiousness, consternation, fretting, worry; they're tormentors. And we're delivered to them because the root of the matter is not taken care of. There's unforgiveness somewhere. And if it's not fully unforgiveness, it's resentment. It's past hurt. It's a seeping wound. It's a misunderstanding of an action. ...That we just don't let it go. Oh we put it over here, but honey, if we get bumped the right way the puss will come out and say, "Oh, here I am."

Take Inventory—Who Do I Need to Forgive?

I'm talking about getting permanent deliverance from fear. We need to take inventory right now. We need to just take inventory. "Who haven't I forgiven?" Oh boy, I'm right on it right now. The bells are ringing. They're here right now. I'm holding something. It could've been thirty years ago that something was said, or done, that made you go the wrong way and you've had that thing and it never has been taken care of. "Am I saved?" Yes you're saved, but you're under the scrutiny of tormentors! And they didn't come from the devil; they came from God. Why? To get you to be aware that something needs to be handled! Why should we pray for the Lord to deliver us from this fear? The fear has been produced by tormentors that have been brought into our lives because we won't handle the root of the matter; and God's not going to lift it off until we do this.

I promise you, if we're hurting here, and if we do this, and this is the root, and we handle all the tentacles that reach over here and to the surface, the root will be cut off. It's the old story of cause and effect, and sowing and reaping. ...I'm not going any further. We are not going until we handle this right now! We need to deal with forgiveness. It's in this Bible! I'm not reading from a comic book, it's in this Bible! You say,
"Well, they didn't do right."
"Well, welcome to the human race."
"Well, they mistreated me and I got the short end of the deal."
"Well, tell that to Jesus, He's hanging on the cross. He knows a little about short ends and deals. He's the one on the cross that says, "Father forgive them they know not what they do."

Want to be Like Jesus—Start With Forgiving Others

If He can forgive people for what they don't know that they do, how much more should we forgive people who knew what they were doing?
"I just want to be like Jesus. I'm gonna to be like Jesus."

Well, here's a good chance to start..."I can't hardly wait until we got revival services with everything jumping and jukin' yea! I'm gonna be like Jesus." ...Well, I'm giving you a chance to be like Jesus right now.
"I want to be just like Jesus."
"You do? Here we are." ...Never did find any scriptures where Jesus talked in tongues.
"I'm going to be like Jesus and talk in tongues."

Peace Born Out of a Forgiving Heart

He didn't talk in tongues. But he did forgive. And he was the
one who said, "My peace I leave thee." Did he give us a putrefying peace? Did he give us an annoyed peace? Did he give us a peace that had all kinds of foolishness in it? Did we get an impure peace, or did we get a full peace? He said, "My peace I leave thee. My peace I give unto thee not as the world giveth, give I unto thee." What kind of peace did He give us? ...A kind of peace that is born out of a heart that knows how to forgive.

Forgive and Forget!

The scripture says, "Likewise shall my heavenly father do also unto you. If ye not from your hearts forgive not every one his brother their trespass." We got to forgive and then we got to forget it and go on.
"Well I got a raw deal."
"Tough break!"
"Well, they cheated me."
"Well, I've been cheated too!"

If I had all the money people stole from me I could take a trip around the world for free. You think I'm going to stay up at night and count my nickels and dimes and quarters and bad things that have been said about me? That's a bunch of bologna! I'm just going to go on. It's back to the old analogy of the person that cuts out in front of you, and while they drive down the street you're giving them Cain...and they got their back to you! Three blocks, you're havin' indigestion and they're looking for something to chew on...has no idea what's going on in your head. You've got acid indigestion and he's going to go and have a steak and potato. That's great!

And so it is; sometimes when you don't forgive...the person you haven't forgiven—they sleep well...you're staring at the ceiling..."You dirty blah, blah, blah.... Hope you get AIDS, you dirty blah, blah, blah...." Come on, its Bible study. Some of you that I'm looking at -- your silence is deafening. You look at me as if to say, "I wonder who he's ministering to." I wish 'they' were here.

Forgiveness. You ought to take inventory. You're going to have to take it because you'll never...I'll pray over you and pray for you and council you and deal with you, but God will not even let me get from home plate to first base with you. It's just like the Holy Ghost says, "Nope, there's an issue here. Stop." "There's a diagnosis here that needs to be taken care of right here." "There's something that's not forgiven here." "There's just a feeling of being held here."

You say, "Well Brother Arnold it's hard." Who said it was easy? Just a matter if you want to live in torment, or not. Fear has torment. Scripture says if you don't forgive from your heart, He turns you over to the tormentors, (plural).

Just Let it Go!

There's something else that we need to do to overcome. I'll let it go, because you're going to have to handle it just like I'm going to have to handle it.

I have people that I resent. I have people that I don't like. There are people that I pastor that I don't care much for. And that's not good, either. But there's a difference between personality clashes and character traits that are not good. And there are people that I resent that mock everything I teach and everything I stand for, whose tongues wag on both ends, who, to me, are nothing but a bunch of brain-dead chimpanzees dressed up like humans. Jesus Christ couldn't pastor some of these people. He couldn't do it, because they wouldn't do what He said...because they won't do what I say. And I resent that and I have to fight that all the time, because it's my natural nature to walk up and say, "Hey listen stupid, I've already heard what you said and I've already heard what you did, and I'm tired of it and why don't you just get your hide out of here, ignorant!" "If you're not going to play the way the team plays, get your hide out of here, ignorant!" "I need you like I need leprosy." "Get lost." "Go be a fool somewhere else." "Get lost." That's me, but, you see, I won't ever say that. I won't say that! I'll just bite my tongue and go pray and say, "Lord, make me be like Jesus." I want to be like Jesus.

God's Love Not Predicated on Performance

You do everything you possibly can to help people to get them to be like the Lord; and you're trying to be like the Lord; and you're trying to confess and be pure and transparent, while a bunch of idiots act like a bunch of idiots! Hello? And now the Lord says to me, "Come on and forgive them Jeffery." And I say, "Ah, come on."

If you're not careful and you let the thing brew in you, you'd almost be happy that they'd leave and be lost. You almost just want to say, "Hah, go somewhere else and be lost," and the Lord won't let that happen. He says, "No, you're going to handle it and you're going to help them." And I've told the Lord,
"But I don't even like her. I just don't like her. We don't gel."
"Learn to like her!"
"But she won't do right."

Now watch this, now I'm letting you into some of my prayer time:
"But she won't do right."

And the Lord says, "Right, just like you!" "And I love you and I like you—not predicated on your performance, but the fact that I am Love."

Being Like Jesus is a Journey

Now you can smile all you want to, but I'm right where you is. Now, we all have those feelings and we're lying if we say, "Oh not me." There are some people that we gel with and some people that we just kind of clash with. But whether we gel, we mesh, or we clash, we have to try and be like Jesus Christ. It takes an effort. You don't just receive the beautiful gift of the Holy Ghost and all of a sudden, "Oh, just like Jesus." No you're not. You find out the more you try to be like the Lord, if you're honest, the more you discover you're worse off then when you weren't trying to be like the Lord.

I almost envy some people I've met in the body of Christ, who still are living where they were when they first got into the church. They're right there in Acts 2:38. They've never left Acts 2:38. They're happy there. They're oblivious to everything. They don't know there are any other pastures. They're just right there, they talk in tongues every once in a while, and shake their hands...they're right there. Some of us poor idiots are climbing out...and this stuff of trying to be like Him...and it seems the closer you get to being like Him the more He reveals how you're not like Him. And if you're heart isn't sincere, it's easy to become discouraged with saying, "Man, I've been this way for fifteen years." "I've been trying to get close to God and now here I almost see more light and I understand more and

I realize how nasty I am." And if you're not careful and you don't take that revelation with a right spirit, you will start resenting the bimbos who are sitting on Acts 2:38, who are just oblivious.

Walk in the Light—It Shows What We Need to Change

And here you are trying to discipline yourself and get rid of these feelings and resentments and these deep things and you say to yourself, "How come ol' ignorant Joe from Kokomo never feels that? How come they don't ever get going anywhere?" It's because they're walking in diminutive light. Watch this now? That's why so many people in so-called Christian circles are not condemned, or either convicted by so many things that we hold so dear to our hearts...because their light is small.

What does the Bible say in John? "Light makes manifest." You have a little bit of light and you can see a little bit of junk. If God gives you more light you can see a whole lot of junk. If you start walking in the light...my God! That's why the Bible says, "Walk in the light as He is in the light, we have fellowship in Him and His blood cleanses us from all unrighteousness and sinfulness and uncleanness" as we walk in the light.

What is He saying? ...As we walk deeper in the things of God you begin to see how pure and holy He really is and how cruddy you really are, and how desperately you need the washing and the mercy and the cleansing and the bathing of the blood of Jesus. And that means you're not satisfied with just a few hundred people and a nice little hair-do and a nice little auditorium. There's something burning and churning and yearning in you wanting to know, "When do I get to be like you?" "When do I get to stop being resentful and unforgiving and unkind and crude?" "I want to be like you." Somehow the Holy Ghost gently says, "Well, just keep on walking." "Walk." "Walk." "Walk in the light." "For with light you shall see life."

The Deep Things of God is Brighter Light

I'm talking about getting rid of fear. Some of us are not honest with ourselves, so we walk very, very little in light. Why? Light makes manifest! And if people start to discipline themselves and begin to pray and fast and really try to go after the deep things of God...do you know what the deep things of God are? They're not deep dark secrets. They're bright light! And if we start going after the deep things of God, it's bright light. And when you start walking in bright light, you'll notice how cruddy you are.

You were all right back there in Acts 2:38, in just your little diminutive light. And say all you want to, I'm not trying to be rude to our forefathers, I thank God for the heritage that we have, but for forty years we've been at Acts 2:38. And there's a whole bunch of Bible past Acts 2:38 to help us grow.

So you don't walk away saying, "The guy's gone whacko." No, I don't think there's any other New Birth message other than Acts 2:38. That's the only one that I know how to get in...repentance, water baptism in Jesus name, the gift of the Holy Ghost. I don't know of any other entrance way.

To Overcome Fear Fill Mind With Thoughts of God

But for us to stay there is dangerous and causes us to live in fear. You understand what I'm saying? Okay, If we're going to get permanent victory over fear, we have to fill our minds...our minds...with the thoughts of God. Because fear expresses itself as an emotion, it comes through your head—through your head. Even God himself cannot just literally grab a hold of you in your emotional realm and get you saved. He cannot, and will not, do that.

He chooses the foolishness of preaching to save them that believe. And preaching goes through your ear, the sieve of your mind... and then it touches your emotion. That's why a person can walk in church and know nothing about God, and there'll be a sensation of the Holy Ghost and they'll sense and feel something and not know what to do. And that's why the church is there—to instruct.

Direction Needed With Emotional Experience

That's why God had Simon Peter go over and preach to Cornelius; "Faith cometh by hearing and hearing by the Word of God." And when faith came and he heard the preaching: Boom! ...he has an emotional experience and then Simon Peter tells him what it is. "You've just got the Holy Ghost." He didn't know what happened, Peter told him, for he heard them talking in tongues. He said, "These guys have got the Holy Ghost! Where's the water, lets baptize them." Why? He needs direction added to his emotional experience and he's got to talk to the man's mind.

Listen folks, God and the devil are after our minds! Both of them. That's right; both of them are after our minds. That's the danger of this transcendental meditation, and this guru stuff, and this eastern religion stuff; it's mind stuff. Does it work? Yes it works! But it circumvents Calvary. It says, "I can be everything God wants me to be without His program and without His blood and without the Lamb." And that's wrong. That's an aborted way to do something. And God will not accept that!

Use Scripture as Preventive Medicine—Not A Cure-all

It's back to Cain and Abel. The Bible says we need to fill our minds with the thoughts of God. Isaiah 26:3, "Thou will keep him in perfect peace whose mind is stayed upon thee for he trusteth in thee." You know why sometimes our minds aren't on the Lord? Come on, we're going to be honest tonight…because we don't trust Him until our resources fail.

"For he trusteth in thee." Many times when we finally fill our minds with the Word of God, it's when we're so full of fear and consternation and frustration…honey, you can't even hardly believe. Don't you understand what this means? Sometimes we use scriptures as a cure-all and a catch-all for a situation. This thing is preventive medicine. If we would live by these Biblical principles daily, there wouldn't be any big catastrophes.

You don't see Paul or Silas in their jail just going into a fit and a rage and a thirty-day fast and all that stuff. Man, them dudes start singing! You don't see anything in Acts 16 where they say, "Man, we better get a hold of God now!" They don't do anything like that. God has saved that for you and me. Come on now. We done it lots of times…"Oh we got to get a hold of God now…." Well, what did you have a hold of the last three days?

Listen to me. I know powerful men that live in the Spirit that blow me away, because they're never wiped out. I mean, death can come, and sickness can come…disaster can come and they walk with the same stride. They say, "Well, lets just take care of this, Jesus?" And they walk away and have it taken care of and you're going, "Aren't you going to get sweaty?" No, because they live in the light, and so it's just easy to function.

Don't Live Borderline

You see, we live borderline; just enough to ease conscience, just enough to get by with me.... And then when a little bit of Hell happens, we're trying to find Heaven. Where, if we would just change the tables and just live in Heaven daily, what could Hell do to Heaven?

It's like...they brought the message to Jesus and said, "Hey, you better get out of town man, Herod's after your carcass!" You notice Jesus just said: Tell that old fox...that uh, I do cures today and tomorrow, and on the third day I'll be glorified.

Now his disciples are going...but Jesus is just saying: You tell that old fox.... You ever wonder why he called Herod a fox? Because a fox is only king of the chicken coop! He don't do very well with lions. And the fox just sent a note to the lion. And the lion just turned around and said: Tell the chicken coop-king to cool it.

Honey, you got the lion inside you. We don't have to be sneaky and foxy and try to...we got the lion of the tribe of Judah inside of us. We need to fill our minds with the law of the lion of the tribe of Judah, rather than that stupid old lion that goes around trying to roar and scare us. The Bible never did say the devil was a lion. He said he goes about "as" a lion. That means he's an imposter! But Jesus ain't an imposter! He's the real lion!

Fill Your Mind With Thoughts of God

Fill our minds with the thoughts of God. That's why Romans 12:1&2 says, "I beseech you therefore"... I beg you, I implore you, I plead with you... "I beseech you by the mercies of God present your bodies a living sacrifice wholly and acceptable unto the Lord." Why is Paul saying that to saints? To prevent them from sexual misconduct, to prevent them from having conduct that would bring a reproach to the body of Christ. He is giving them preventative medicine.

"Present your bodies a living sacrifice wholly and acceptable unto the Lord which is your reasonable service"...he's not asking something unreasonable. That's reasonable... "and don't be conformed to this world but be transformed by the renewing of your minds." How do you renew your minds? You renew your minds in the presence of His Spirit and the presence of His Word.

Quality Over Quantity in Scripture Reading

When you read a scripture, you don't have to read dozens and dozens of chapters, if you would just read a verse, or two, or three. And stop and say, "Holy Spirit of the living God, let me receive the nutrition and the medicine and the power from this scripture." For just one word from God was enough to create the universe and you've got words from God and you've got to just let it get in your MIND so it will introduce peace. In your MIND! I'm concerned that sometimes our scripture reading is quantity and not quality. "Well, I need to read a few chapters."

You may just need to read a few verses! Read a verse and say, "Okay, now, Holy Spirit..."

Fill Your Head With Fear or Faith—Word of the Enemy or Word of God

Now you may think I'm crazy, but this is the way I live. That's why I'm crazy. This is the way I live. I talk to the

Holy Spirit of God. "Now Holy Ghost talk to me." "Show me what this means." "Bring it out to me." "Make me understand." Sometimes it'll go *wheeew*, and sometimes I don't have anything! I don't feel any quickening. I'll read some more scripture and I'll ask the Holy Ghost, "Let this scripture be with me during the day." "Bring it to my remembrance." "Let it come inside me." "Bring it to me." There is life in this thing. My God, man, you can't be thinking about the same thing, two different things at the same time...you can't do that. You either got to fill your head with fear, or faith. You got to fill your head with the Word of God, or the word of the enemy; one or the other.

Be Transformed by Renewing Mind

Now you may be a big-brain dude, but your brain ain't that big! You can't have both of them. ..."Be ye transformed." That means changed, metamorphosed. You know...caterpillar...cocoon...to butterfly...changed by the renewing of your mind. "Ing", renew*ing*; active, active verb. Not past tense; active. Renewing...process. ..."That you might prove what's the good and perfect and acceptable will of God."
"Oh, I only wish that I could get the will of God."
It's within your brain....
"I'm going to move away. I'm going to go here, or join this, or that."

You're crazy, man! You could do it right here. Right here. You can renew your mind and prove what is the good and perfect, acceptable will of God. And when God lets you know that will, *then* maybe it is your will to go here and do this, or that: but we're moving, we're like gypsies for Jesus. We're all the time moving every which way, turning here and there...and it can be settled *here*.

Full of Holy Ghost Energy, But Frustrated

I've preached in Bible schools across this nation. I've preached in conferences across this nation. I've preached youth conventions across this nation. We've got a generation of frustrated kids who are full of energy and they do have the Holy Ghost and they do have a zeal for God; and no direction.
"What am I going to do?"
"Stop, meditate, read, and wait. Wait."

It would be embarrassing right here, right now, in this auditorium, if I asked for a show of hands; and I'm not, so don't do it; if I asked for a show of hands, "In the last three days how many have heard the voice of God?" "I mean, in the last three days God has just come by and talked to you? Just talked to you? Quickened things to you and made you to understand Him? Talk to you?" 99.9% of us here would go; "Uhhh." "I thought you had the Holy Ghost? How do you recognize the voice of God?"

That's where our problem is. And that's why many movements are far out-growing us. "Do they have all the truth?" No, I don't think so. "Do they have some truth?" Yes. "They got the Holy Ghost?" Yes. "Well how come...?" They're hearing from God. They're walking in what light they have.

Think on These Things....

Paul wrote to the Philippian church and said, "Whatsoever things are true, whatsoever things are honest, whatsoever things are just, pure, lovely, good report, any virtue, any praise, think on these things." Some of us would be better off not reading the newspaper, or watching the television. I never have and I don't understand to this day, and maybe

I'm an idiot, but I don't understand some of you people saying, "I just have a television, because I want to watch the news."

If I watched the news and listened to it I could become suicidal. You just filled your head and your heart with an hour of total rape, murder, desecration, devastation, hopelessness...and you walked and turned the TV off and said, "Oh, I feel better now that I know what's going on around me." And then you say, "You know, that stuff doesn't bother me. I could go lay down right now. It doesn't bother me at all."

God's Word—From Your Eyes & Ears to Your Heart

Okay, Proverbs 4:20, I'm going to show you something else we need to do to overcome fear permanently: "My son attend to my words and incline thine ear unto my sayings." Listen. "Let them not depart from thine eyes; keep them in the midst of thine heart." Now, he just told you the two keys to get the peace of God in you. It's the ear-gate and the eye-gate. "For they are life unto those that find them...." They can't get into your heart until they get through your eyes or your ears! They are life unto those that find them. Now watch this, here's the verse for healing. ..."And health to all their flesh." That's why you get healed by the word of God, because the Word of God is healing and health to their flesh.

God has chosen the eye-gate and the ear-gate and the writer of Proverbs said, "Now listen my boy, keep a hold of my word. Don't let it go." Once again Verse 20: "My son attend to my words; incline thy ear unto my sayings." Incline thine ear! In other words; listen up! Watch. "Let them not depart from thine eyes." Watch what he just said now. Watch! Look! And listen! Why? Because if you look and listen, you'll live, because my words are life. And they are health unto your flesh. ..."Faith cometh by hearing and hearing by the word of God." Amen? Then fear comes by hearing and hearing by the word of the devil! Fear and faith arrive to everybody by the ear-gate and the eye-gate.

Faith & Fear—Both From Seeing & Hearing

Moses told Israel in Deuteronomy 4, "Ye have seen what the Lord has done to the Egyptians. How he has broken the power of Pharaoh." You know what He told Joshua about taking the land in Jericho, and not to be afraid. He said, "You have seen his presence...and you have heard his voice." He was trying to tell them that you ought to have faith and not be afraid. Why? Because you've seen and heard. You've seen and heard! And what ever you see or hear produces fear or faith, depending on how you perceive it.

Deuteronomy 4:9, "Only take heed to thyself and keep thy soul diligently, lest thou forget the things which thine eyes have seen, and lest they depart from thy heart all the days of thy life"...because you can forget what you've seen and heard... "but teach them thy sons, and thy sons' sons." Verse 10, "Specially the day that thou stoodest before the Lord thy God in Ho'-reb, when the Lord said unto me, gather me the people together, and I will make them hear my words, that they may learn to fear me all the days that they shall live upon the earth"...that's Godly reverence... "And that they may teach their children. And ye came near and stood unto the mountain; and the mountain burned with fire unto the midst of the heaven"...wait a minute! They saw the fire? They saw the Holy smoke? ..."With darkness, clouds, and thick darkness. And the

Lord spake unto you out of the midst of the fire: ye heard the voice of the words"...and they heard the voice?

Faith Should Grow From What's Seen & Heard of God

Now watch what happened. They saw, and they heard. It should have created faith, but they saw other things that created fear...giants and walled cities and problems... "But saw no similitude; only ye heard a voice." Now did you hear what I just said? Some of us here right now, your faith and your tranquility ought to be so gigantic, because of things you have seen in your lifetime. I mean, you have seen God pick people out of the sewer and just turn their lives around, including yourself. You have seen a demonstration of the power of God, and you have heard great preaching, and great teaching, and diverse preaching, and diverse teaching, and you've heard great singing, and you've heard choirs and quartets, and you've heard the gifts of the Spirit operating here, and you have felt the witness of the Holy Ghost inside you. If there's anybody in this city that ought to have peace, and tranquility, and faith, and soundness of thought and mind, it ought to be this family!! We ought not to demonstrate to the world worry, and consternation, and apprehension, when you think of what you've seen!

Some of the messages that God has given in this church...I don't give a good flip if none of you believe them. I believe them and God believes them. I've had missionaries call me and write me letters and told me...one in particular, in person and he's a spiritual man; he said, "I've never in all my life heard such awesome tongues and interpretations as in the few nights that I was with you." "I've never felt anything like it." "I've never heard a thing like it."

Now, I'll tell you what my friend, you have heard and seen and felt things. And you need to fight to keep them in your hearts lest the devil steal them away from you in a moment of frenzied fear and you say, "I don't think it was God." I'm a telling you, it was God!

We need to rehearse it over and over and over and over. Some of the messages I've heard…my God, man, I mean…a-shakin' and a-quakin' in my body—like electricity! …Fear of the Lord that just swept in when some of these fellows would give that interpretation, or that message…my hair would stand up. My Spirit would say, "This is God."

Say what you want to about all our standards and rules and regulations, I don't know if we're right or wrong on all of them. We're trying to get a proper direction. But I know our doctrine is right and I know our message is right and I know that the Word of God is right. I know it's right! Nobody can steal it from me. And I find myself, sometimes, I've got to fight with that spirit of doubt and fear that says, "Well maybe it wasn't God." It was God! You can't let that spirit of doubt, and fear, and worry, rape your soul and say, "Well that maybe was, or wasn't." That's why Moses told his people, "Lest you forget." Keep it alive. Keep it alive, because the spirit of fear will give birth to unbelief. It will give birth to doubt.

The following is a record of the interpretation of two messages in tongues given at conclusion of Bro. Arnold's teaching. They are included for your blessing and benefit although they are specific to the church in Gainesville

(First Tongues and Interpretation)

Fear: it entereth in like a growth. It entereth in under your body. It gets to grow and grow and grow until it becomes something that must be operated on. It grows until it brings pressure. It grows until it cannot be contained. Just this way it is growing in your hearts. It is growing. You cannot contain it. You cannot hold it. It has become immeasurable. It has become impossible. But I, I the Lord God will reach unto you. I will perform upon you those things that are necessary to decrease this monster inside and bring it back to its right size in your eyes, that you look upon it and you don't fear. You look upon it and there's peace in your hearts. You look upon it and that perfect love shines within your heart. I, the Lord God, will operate upon you. I will work upon your heart and upon your mind and bring to you the comfort and the joy and the peace that you desire. Seek Me. Look unto Me. Believe My words for they are Light. Believe My words for they are Comfort. Believe My words for they are Peace.

(Second Tongues and Interpretation)

For ye have carried it too long. Ye have tried to live yourself with pain you can't control. You have not looked unto Me and trusted in Me. But I would that you would reach unto Me. Look unto Me now. Reach unto Me now. Take My word that my servant hath given unto you. Take it unto your hearts. Take it as a medicine. Take it into yourselves that you would overcome. That this thing that has become so big to you, that it would begin to decrease in size. I, the Lord God, minister unto you now. I minister unto you in this moment. For I love you. I love you. You are dear unto Me. You are my child. I would not have you to fear. I would not have you to have this torment within you, but I would deliver you. I would set you free this night now and sbreak the bonds and the chains that are holding you and the fears that are holding you back. I will deliver you now in this hour. Reach unto Me now.

Bro. Arnold's closing remarks

We have a promise from God that right now the Lord said He'd heal every one of us. He'd loose every one of us. If we'd let go. If we would just trust. He called it a medicine. You need the medicine. Now, take it right now. Give it over to Him. Release yourself to the wisdom and the will of the great surgeon, the great physician who wants to heal you right now. Some of you are hurting very deep right now in your hearts and in your spirits. Come on, the Lord has come and He said, "I would heal you right now."

Order Information

Please call us, or see our web site at www.gainesvilleupc.net for the most current listing of all books in print by Rev. Jeff Arnold, including:

***"The Why & Wonder Of Worship Book One-
Volumes One, Two & Three"***

***"The Why & Wonder Of Worship Book Two-
The Final Series"***

(all six volumes now in two books, transcribed as Rev. Arnold taught on the subject of Worship)

"Five More Minutes"
(many years of inspiring Sunday Bulletin articles)

"The Pulpit Of Pastor Jeff Arnold"
In text, a Computer CD-Rom in PDF format containing
"The Why & Wonder Of Worship Book One"
"Five More Minutes"

"Pulpit Notes" Volume One
Volume Two
(a written record, ideal for study, of the high points in the teachings of Rev. Arnold from selected subjects; a continuing series)

AND WATCH FOR THE RELEASE OF:
"God Is Building Himself a House"

CHECK WITH US PERIODICALLY FOR NEW TITLES

THE PENTECOSTALS OF GAINESVILLE
TRUTH PUBLICATIONS
8105 NW 23rd Avenue
Gainesville, FL 32606
PHONE: (352) 376-6320 FAX: (352) 376-7105
www.gainesvilleupc.net